UN-CONSCIOUS-CITY
WIEL ARETS

00:00:00 –
01:12:00

UNCONSCIOUS

PROCESSING PERCEPTION, MEMORY, LEARNING, THOUGHT, AND LANGUAGE WITHOUT AWARENESS.

PROMPTER

Wiel, when did you first become interested in the 'un', in regards to the act of being unconscious? It is the foundation of what we are calling, and what we are about to discuss: the Unconscious City.

THE ARCHITECT

When I first began studying, I originally choose to focus on physics. I did this because I believed that physics had to do with the unknown, the uncertain, and even the unconscious. Many things are still unknown, or have an unknown outcome. The first man on the Moon, for instance, or the robot; these developments led to unknown destinations, with unknown potential for further discoveries. The idea of the unknown is something that I've been interested in for a very long time. Yet once I made the decision to begin studying architecture, and when I was confronted with my architecture professors, it only took me three weeks to realize that I had to go to the library, because my professors were lecturing in an omniscient way.

PROMPTER

Does that mean you enjoy the potential to discover, which seems to be endlessly possible in libraries because of their seemingly limitless amount of knowledge? The ways in which we use a library reminds me of a rhizome structure, with no hierarchy, enabling its users to go in any possible direction, without knowing their destination.

'...the rhizome connects any point to any other point, and its traits are not necessarily linked to traits of the same

nature; it brings into play very different regimes of signs, and even nonsign states... It is composed not of units but of dimensions, or rather directions in motion. It has neither beginning nor end, but always a middle (milieu) from which it grows and which it overspills... The rhizome proceeds by variation, expansion, conquest, capture, off-shoots. Unlike the graphic arts, drawing or photography, unlike tracings, the rhizome pertains to a map that... is always detachable, connectable, reversible, modifiable, and has multiple entryways and exits and its own lines of flight.'

—Gilles Deleuze and Félix Guattari, *A Thousand Plateaus: Capitalism and Schizophrenia* (Minneapolis: University of Minnesota Press, 1987), 23.

PROMPTER

How would you, then, describe your relationship with your professors during your studies, especially considering that the role has been reversed, and today you are a professor yourself?

THE ARCHITECT

I think that professors should ask questions instead of giving answers, which tend to limit thoughts. That's the reason to be in the academic world: to question and research. I did that while I was a student. I went to the library and felt that I had to ask myself my own questions. During the rest of my studies I was always reading, buying many books, and writing quite a lot within them. For me, my books are a kind of mirror. In school I always presented my doubts and questions to my professors, but having a debate with them was not always easy. There were of course, exceptions to this.

When I began to teach, I always knew that as a professor I was also a student. As a professor, you have the chance to search for an answer, and the answer always implies the next question. I've followed this strategy throughout my numerous professorships.

In the book *Wiel Arets: Autobiographical References*, there are many question marks, a lot of unknowns, and much insecurity. That has to do with the insecurity that an architect, in my opinion, should have. Of course sometimes you follow a strategy that defines the next steps and therefore acts as a frame for a certain period of time. But the unsecured, especially the 'un', has had monumental meaning for me, for quite some time. I would never say, 'I know.' I want to always question everything. That's why I always, as a professor, say, 'I am the same as you. I would like to be part of this debate.'

PROMPTER

The 'un' describes something that cannot be seen or has not yet been discovered, and it implies the acknowledgement of the opposite. Hence it always requires a confrontation, which makes us realize its value and consequences. Are you implying what interests you about the 'un', is absence?

00:09:00

THE ARCHITECT

When I look to the most beautiful woman, she actually becomes interesting only when she no longer looks as perfect as she at first seemed. Interesting women, for me, are not those who are seemingly perfect. Interesting begins when something doesn't work. The 'un' makes you wonder, ponder, and question.

PROMPTER

How do you relate this to the Unconscious City? It makes me think of introducing conflicts into a city, which might have a rather negative connotation, but it could potentially unfold qualities within cities that otherwise would not be seen without them.

THE ARCHITECT

I speak about the Unconscious City now, because in former generations European societies anticipated planning. When one made a building then, it had to be made exactly like *this*, for instance. It had to be beautiful, and so on. But today, we all understand that it's maybe more interesting to go to a city that's 1,000 years old, rather than visit a brand new one, such as Dubai. I am fascinated by the idea of change and decay. I am not interested in perfection, nor am I so much interested in utopias, but I am interested in what is happening in the world right now. We can wonder, we can speculate, and we can take an interest in philosophy, but at the end of the day, I will always ask myself: 'What do we do now?'

PROMPTER

Isn't a utopia also a speculation, but connected to a specific place?

Definition of Utopia:
1: an imaginary and indefinitely remote place

00:11:15

2: often capitalized: a place of ideal perfection especially in laws, government, and social conditions
3: an impractical scheme for social improvement

THE ARCHITECT

When you read utopian ideas, people always write quite specifically: what will happen next? Speculation means that things might go in a certain direction, or they might not. I think this is much more interesting, because we invite everyone to consider how the future might develop. The Americans John Mauchly and John Presper Eckert, who created the world's first general purpose, electronic, digital programmable computer, once stated that everyone would have a computer room in their house. And this is, of course, not true. Today, my phone is a million times smarter than that first computer in 1943, the Electronic Numerical Integrator and Computer (ENIAC). And within this book we will speculate about what may happen next, to cities. We will speculate how the human being might change. And how apparatuses might be developed. But I choose not to go much further than that.

PROMPTER

Does this mean your own speculations are very consciously chosen?

THE ARCHITECT

I think that in a very short period of time, the GPS will make our transport systems very different from what they are now. But instead of saying this, I believe that we have to communicate these speculations through statements about, for instance, a changing 'ground level' in cities. I believe the GPS and electronic cars – that is, cars that are driverless – will help us make transport in the city smarter, and change our cities to a great extent.

Imagine if there were no noise in the city anymore. No pollution. No traffic jams. This would have a dramatic effect on cities.

PROMPTER

Which role does the perception of a changing society play in city dwelling? The demands on a city vary according to the changes people in that specific city are grappling with. I am trying to think which needs would rise from the absence of the familiar city noises. What impact would this have on our built environment?

THE ARCHITECT

As architects and urban planners we should talk much more about how people perceive the city. That is why we have cities: for people to live in them, to walk in them, to meet in both the private and public realms, which I believe have to be thought about from the issue of interiority. And these people living in cities, during the next couple of years, will change them in an incredible way through external forces. These forces will change our perception. I believe not only in physical changes of cities, but also in our varying perceptions of them. While the building itself may have changed very little, the culture, life surrounding it, has. Different knowledge is available today than there was a century ago. People have simply changed. And I believe, alongside the changes to our built environment, that people will change, or adapt, too. Hence the effect on people depends on their own ability to change. How people will change, I do not know. But within all this change, we have to understand that stylistic aspects, such as how a façade looks, are secondary. Perception changes because of knowledge, and because of themes that are currently in debate, such as those about the ways in which newspapers, television, and all other media brainwash the majority of the world's population.

'Interiority is a term we can use to express architecture's

ability to give a sense of space that rules out an exterior. We think verbally about our perception of moving in public space or inside a building, but also of reading a book or watching a film. Interiority is a term we use to describe the intellectual and emotional multidimensionality of all named disciplines.'

—Wiel Arets, 2008

PROMPTER

I ask myself where stylistic aspects begin and to what extent they are an important part of defining places to meet. Recognizing stylistic aspects as secondary, what relevance does technology have within architecture?

THE ARCHITECT

Le Corbusier compared the house with a machine during the Industrial Revolution; today we don't know what to compare our houses to. Certainly now that the world has become more virtual, or digital, as opposed to physical. We must realize that digital technology is invisible and that we use it unconsciously, just as we use buildings and cities unconsciously. Every city, is an Unconscious City. The moment we understand that, we can begin to manipulate and speculate as to how we might change the city, or make a new one. This is only speculation, but it can be very powerful to realize that this could have a great impact on the physical world to come. Style has no part in these debates. Style has to do with control. This relates to how the cities of Barcelona and Tokyo have been, and are being, developed.

PROMPTER

Architects have the potential to be very powerful. What is the most effective way to pursue these speculations?

THE ARCHITECT

Architects are not recognized walking down the street. They are not heroes. The architect is not a looming figure in today's society. Actually, architects have not designed most of the buildings within a city; developers have. Developers have a much larger impact on cities than the architect. The only thing left to do, is to develop a strategy, to circumvent this situation, which may be abstract. Most of the houses on Amsterdam's canals were not designed by architects; they were built by contractors. They are individual houses that make the urban realm of the canals look great.

Definition of Strategy:
An adaptation or complex of adaptations (as of behavior, metabolism, or structure) that serves or appears to serve an important function in achieving evolutionary success

THE ARCHITECT

I believe that the development of a strategy can have an overwhelming effect. Early-twentieth century architects had political aspirations, since their collective attitude of sharing went beyond their buildings themselves. It was shared interest of a new progressive lifestyle. The collective ambiance of the spirit that was then in the air in dance, film, photography, music, industrial design, fashion, architecture, literature and philosophy, amongst others, are representative of that era. And what we can learn from

that is that we must always be aware of the present moment. When the Modern Movement held conferences and declared the International Style, it had an enormous influence on 'the building', as well as urban design. And maybe even more so on industrial design, and for sure, society at large. And their ideas are still incredible today. Among many other things they thought about, for instance, were new building techniques, the role of the sun, questioning the ornament, and so on. These aspects are all very physical and tangible; similar to today's digital-physical condition.

PROMPTER

We should develop strategies, but with regard to the invisible integration of technology. Consequently, the relationship of our physical world, the invisible character of recent technology, and the unconscious perception of people living in cities, must be taken into account. Bringing these different parameters, such as form, technology, and people, into a relationship with one another, reminds me of something I read on the British Sociological Association's website:

'In order to survive human beings must extract materials from their environment. Generically this is referred to as production. People in societies have devised forms of organization and methods of technology which facilitate and potentiate the process.'

—'What do Sociologists do?', *British Sociological Association*

00:22:30

PROMPTER

To which other disciplines that use the unconsciousness as a strategic device, do you relate?

THE ARCHITECT

Everyone perceives unconsciously. When you watch a movie, you don't think about the script. The film unravels itself to you; Godard made me conscious of this condition. There are two important film directors I admire, among others: Eisenstein and Godard. Eisenstein understood that when one makes a movie, emotion is the most important tool. All of his movies were emotional cuts. Scenes were stitched together to evoke an emotion. Godard, rather, produced an intellectual montage. He placed three or four shots in sequences, and partly overlapping in such a way that they wouldn't necessarily be understood. He used color and quotes, but also added stills of advertisements in-between film sequences. The brain would process the input, but not consciously. This was the first time that I experienced the power of the unconscious.

This subtle transfer reminds me of the songlines of the Indigenous Australians, where information is passed from one group to another through song. I like that notion very much, since they created non-physical formal maps. Information in songlines is, on one hand, based on tradition, but on the other, on physical encounters. They allow for independency. What are our dependencies today?

Dependencies explain that people are lonesome. By free will, Valéry said, we are liberated; we can work and do our own thing. The songlines story communicates that since we are not dependent, we are able to move freely and change position within our respective framework.

'Definition of Songlines: A path across the land (or, the sky)

00:24:45

that marks the route followed by an Aboriginal ancestor, which is made during the "Dreaming" and is often recorded in songs, stories, dance, and painting.

PROMPTER

How do you include that unconscious experience in your buildings?

THE ARCHITECT

That's extremely difficult to answer with words. But I would say to develop a cinematographic experience. It's an art I've been trying to master in my buildings over the last twenty years. Within the Academy of Art & Architecture, in Maastricht, there is only one entrance, for what is actually a complex of three buildings. People enter the building and go past the auditorium, library, then they pass the bar, walk over a bridge, past the architecture department, the fashion department, the painters, and the woodshop, including its outdoor courtyard for sculpture—and people traverse this route five times a day. When walking past an artist in that school, his painting will change since last passing by, yet this observer has also changed during the same time period. In the beginning, people complained, and asked why I hadn't created a shortcut. I conceived these short encounters as scenes in a movie. I am also interested in delays, in resistance, and in roughness. The idea of the unconscious was, in retrospect, already in that building. And I've worked with this idea since my very first projects and writings. The idea of the unconscious is something I am constantly grappling with.

PROMPTER

I once read a quote by Colin Rowe, in which he stated that architecture books and theorists who write them, can be divided into two

that marks the route followed by an Aboriginal ancestor, which is made during the "Dreaming" and is often recorded in songs, stories, dance, and painting.'

PROMPTER

How do you include that unconscious experience in your buildings?

THE ARCHITECT

That's extremely difficult to answer with words. But I would say to develop a cinematographic experience. It's an art I've been trying to master in my buildings over the last twenty years. Within the Academy of Art & Architecture, in Maastricht, there is only one entrance, for what is actually a complex of three buildings. People enter the building and go past the auditorium, library, then they pass the bar, walk over a bridge, past the architecture department, the fashion department, the painters, and the woodshop, including its outdoor courtyard for sculpture – and people traverse this route five times a day. When walking past an artist in that school, his painting will change since last passing by, yet this observer has also changed during the same time period. In the beginning, people complained, and asked why I hadn't created a shortcut. I conceived these short encounters as scenes in a movie. I am also interested in delays, in resistance, and in roughness. The idea of the unconscious was, 'in retrospect', already in that building. And I've worked with this idea since my very first projects and writings. The idea of the unconscious is something I am constantly grappling with.

PROMPTER

I once read a quote by Colin Rowe, in which he stated that architecture books and theorists who write them, can be divided into two

distinct groups: the hedgehogs and the foxes. The hedgehog makes a point that's very clear and specific. And so most of the time, they turn out to be wrong, because it's impossible to foresee the future in such a way. An example of such would be the American and his ideas surrounding the future of the computer room. He made a clear statement, yet he failed. The other type would be the fox and they are not very specific in their statements. They often only remark about other people's statements, or stay quite vague. Most of the time they are right, in terms of foreseeing the future, because it's hard to define what their statement actually was, or is. Of course, in a way, the foxes are very smart. And the books that they produce are often more interesting to read than those written by hedgehogs, even though not everything that they expect to happen, actually does, either.

To which character would you refer your own method of working, that of the hedgehog, or the fox?

'"The fox knows many things but the hedgehog knows one big thing." This in the area of our concern, is the statement, otherwise uninteresting, which, in *The Hedgehog and the Fox*, Isaiah Berlin chose to gloss and to elaborate. Taken figuratively

but not pressed too far, what one is supposed to have here are the types of two psychological orientations and temperaments, the one, the hedgehog, concerned with the primacy of the single idea and the other, the fox, preoccupied with multiplicity of stimulus; and the great ones of the Earth divide fairly equally: Plato, Dante, Dostoevsky, Proust, are, needless to say, hedgehogs; Aristotle, Shakespeare, Pushkin, Joyce are foxes. This is the rough discrimination; but if it is representatives of literature and philosophy who are Berlin's critical concern, the game may be played in other areas also. Picasso, a fox, Mondrian, a hedgehog, the figures begin to leap into place; and, as we turn to architecture, the answers are almost entirely predictable. Palladio is a

but not pressed too far, what one is supposed to have here are the types of two psychological orientations and temperaments, the one, the hedgehog, concerned with the primacy of the single idea and the other, the fox, preoccupied with multiplicity of stimulus; and the great ones of the Earth divide fairly equally: Plato, Dante, Dostoevsky, Proust, are, needless to say, hedgehogs; Aristotle, Shakespeare, Pushkin, Joyce are foxes. This is the rough discrimination; but if it is representatives of literature and philosophy who are Berlin's critical concern, the game may be played in other areas also. Picasso, a fox, Mondrian, a hedgehog, the figures begin to leap into place; and, as we turn to architecture, the answers are almost entirely predictable. Palladio is a

hedgehog, Giulio Romano a fox; Hawksmoor, Soane, Philip Webb are probably hedgehogs; Wren, Nash, Norman Shaw almost certainly foxes; and closer to the present day, while Wright is unequivocally a hedgehog, Lutyens is just as obviously a fox... For if Gropius, Mies, Hannes Meyer, Buckminster Fuller are clearly eminent hedgehogs, then where are the foxes whom we can enter in the same league? The preference is obviously one way. The "single central vision" prevails. One notices a predominance of hedgehogs; but, if one might sometimes feel that fox propensities are less than moral and, therefore, not to be disclosed, of course there still remains the job of assigning to Le Corbusier his own particular slot...'

—Colin Rowe and Fred Koetter, *Collage City* (Cambridge: MIT Press, 1978), 91-92.

THE ARCHITECT

I believe in speculations about the development of cities and public realms, and I also believe in the potential changes surrounding the ways in which we live. We should be precise, clear, and provocative. Le Corbusier put two things next to each other: the car and the house. These objects suddenly became very clear. I also have images like this in my mind, and I sometimes bring them to life and show them as slides in my lectures. Images strengthen an idea and can be used as progressive devices. A 'device' is a type of force, and 'progressive' means that it looks forward. I am not at all interested in looking backward. I am never defending; I am interested in a progressiveness that will allow us to understand how tomorrow could work. I think, in this regard, we can be very precise and provocative. For instance, I believe that in forty years there will be someone, or something, walking on Earth that is purely an electronic apparatus. There will be someone, or something, next to the human being. And we will develop the first version of it. And the day that this apparatus becomes advanced and can think, and even talk to other apparatuses in a language created amongst themselves, and only they know, will then further develop itself, on its own. It will be creative and able to reproduce itself; it will be able to complexly develop prototypes of a continuously evolving artificial human being. I am sure about this.

PROMPTER

Talking about the city, which expectations do you have of it? Does the term 'city' have the same connotation as the terms 'mankind', 'evolution', and 'people'? Behind an interest in the city, there will always be a certain expectation – a certain belief. What is your expectation of the city? And where does it have its roots?

THE ARCHITECT

My interest in the city is rooted in the fact that people are now moving in mass to the world's cities, will continue to, and have been doing so for centuries. Unlike now, in the coming decades,

THE ARCHITECT

I believe in speculations about the development of cities and public realms, and I also believe in the potential changes surrounding the ways in which we live. We should be precise, clear, and provocative. Le Corbusier put two things next to each other: the car and the house. These objects suddenly became very clear. I also have images like this in my mind, and I sometimes bring them to life and show them as slides in my lectures. Images strengthen an idea and can be used as progressive devices. A 'device' is a type of force, and 'progressive' means that it looks forward. I am not at all interested in looking backward. I am never defending; I am interested in a progressiveness that will allow us to understand how tomorrow could work. I think, in this regard, we can be very precise and provocative. For instance, I believe that in forty years there will be someone, or something, walking on Earth that is purely an electronic apparatus. There will be someone, or something, next to the human being. And we will develop the first version of it. And the day that this apparatus becomes advanced, and can think, and even talk to other apparatuses in a language created, amongst themselves, and only they know, will then further develop itself, on its own. It will be creative and able to reproduce itself; it will be able to complexly develop prototypes of a continuously evolving artificial human being. I am sure about this.

PROMPTER

Talking about the city, which expectations do you have of it? Does the term 'city' have the same connotation as the terms 'mankind', 'evolution', and 'people'? Behind an interest in the city, there will always be a certain expectation – a certain belief. What is your expectation of the city? And where does it have its roots?

THE ARCHITECT

My interest in the city is rooted in the fact that people are now moving in mass to the world's cities, will continue to, and have been doing so for centuries. Unlike now, in the coming decades,

nearly everybody will live their lives in a city. I believe that cities will grow tremendously in the next few years, and that the global situation will change because of this. Our infrastructure has to change, in order to allow for unforeseen possibilities. As will our houses, as will our production plants. New typologies will be developed, and we will use them everyday.

Who lives in cities now? People with capital. Money will be an extremely decisive tool, now and in the future. The banks and the big firms will have a fascinating impact on how we will live. There will be devices developed in the near future, by informal institutions that will reshape our lives. Big hotels will be built, offering hotel-like-living. These places will have a huge impact on our lives too. And production will once again take place in the city, because it will be clean – there will be no more smoke such as there was in Europe and North America during the nineteenth century. Private institutions in the USA have traditionally sponsored 'culture'. That will soon happen in Europe, too. Art is already driven by speculation. I am very interested in these phenomena.

In 2012 the government of the Netherlands decided to cut the subsidization of culture. They said, 'If people do not want it, why should we pay for it?' And this is all extremely interesting. Money is a force; there are debates about it all the time. Who pays? The new city will be one of diversity. Not everyone and everything will be the same. Cities will be very individualistic. They will be a collection of neighborhoods, all with specific characteristics. What does that mean? It means that our society will change. Less people will get married at a young age, and more people will be living on their own. These are the people that need cities the most. Of course, there are differences between the cities around the world. Climate, resources, wealth, and geographic preconditions can all help to explain these differences.

'Going around museums and galleries, seeing films, talking to

people, seeing new shops, looking at silly magazines, taking an interest in the activities of people in the street, looking at art, traveling: all these things are not useful, all these things do not help me, do not give me any direct stimulation to help my search for something new. And neither does fashion history. The reason for that is that all these things above already exist. I only can wait for the chance for something completely new to be born within myself.'

—Rei Kawakubo, *System* no. 2, 2013.

PROMPTER

We tend to talk about 'the city' the same way we talk about 'a person'. What is he or she going to do with his or her life? How will 'the city' change in the future?

THE ARCHITECT

You're right; we do. That's also why I use the term Unconscious City. We are not talking about something physical. Each city will develop in its own way. Unforeseen stimuli will determine the outcome, and everyday, will be another day. When we talk about the city, we're speaking about the Unconscious City – it's an abstract idea. In the past, I've traveled to Moscow, Rome,

Rio de Janeiro, Shanghai, Tokyo, and Paris, and countless others – the Unconscious City is the description as to how I perceive cities. It is all about perception. This is the point I'm trying to make with the word interiority. Unconscious and interiority are both states of mind.

'When the great cities of Europe and North America first began to open their undergrounds to the traffic of municipal trains, archaeological digs in the Near and Middle East had already begun to uncover the boundary stones and broken walls of Troy, Nineveh, and Babylon. As Paris, London, New York City, and Berlin became electrified, systematized, and plumbed, the cities of antiquity were brought to life for the first time in thousands of years. But even before the digs of Heinrich Schliemann, Sir Arthur John Evans, and Robert Koldewey had substantiated myths and legends from Homer and Genesis, Charles Baudelaire had postulated that

modernity was basically a perceptual faculty that consisted of regarding a modern city—rising outward, upward, and downward on the accumulated wealth of industry and empire—as if it were already ancient. To be modern Baudelaire implies, means to see one's life in a city like Paris poised on the very edge of history, but also in eternity. To be modern requires nerve.

As the languages and cities of Mesopotamia, Egypt, and the Aegean became accessible to the electric lights of modern archaeologists, it became possible to consider Babylonians, Mycenaeans, and Trojans in an oddly familiar way. After the devastations of World War I, Paul Valéry mused, "We later civilizations. . . we too now know that we are mortal. . . Elam, Nineveh,

modernity was basically a perceptual faculty that consisted of regarding a modern city—rising outward, upward, and downward on the accumulated wealth of industry and empire—as if it were already ancient. To be modern Baudelaire implies, means to see one's life in a city like Paris poised on the very edge of history, but also in eternity. To be modern requires nerve.

As the languages and cities of Mesopotamia, Egypt, and the Aegean became accessible to the electric lights of modern archaeologists, it became possible to consider Babylonians, Mycenaeans, and Trojans in an oddly familiar way. After the devastations of World War I, Paul Valéry mused, "We later civilizations... we too now know that we are mortal... Elam, Nineveh,

Babylon were but beautiful vague names, and the total ruin of those work had as little significance for us as their very existence. But France, England, Russia... these too would be beautiful names." Indeed, as European culture began to feel a strange interest in, and identity with, the fallen cities of Mesopotamia and the Nile, a different light was cast on its own cities, both classical and modern. Athens and Rome could never have the same uncovering of Knossos and Babel: it was as if the very ground beneath them were crumbling.'

—Philip Kuberski, 'Unconscious Cities', *The Georgia Review* 44, no. 4 (Winter 1990): 678-679.

THE ARCHITECT

Where are you? You are in the city, the world, and within history. When humans are extinct, there will be no more world, because no one – in the traditional human sense – will be able to perceive it. We are living in a time where our interiority is shaped by the overload of information that we constantly receive. Who provides us with this information? The media. What is media? Schools, universities, TV, mobile devices, etc. But walking through a forest

00:47:15

is also a way to gather information. Is that media? If people stop to walk in the forest, they often have no clue about the flora and fauna surrounding them. Or biodiversity. How are humans supposed to talk about biodiversity if they are unable to distinguish between a rabbit and a hare? Or even between a hedgehog and a fox? When I've walked through the Amazon, I was never able to control my surroundings. In the city, we seem to be able to control everything. We seem to, and we believe we are. But just who is controlling it? Who is in charge? Earlier it was a president or a mayor, but now who is in charge? The modern human being is free, at least that is what he thinks. And this is why we must also speak about interiority. The idea of an exterior is a strange one, because humans are only able to perceive interiors. The forest canopy is an interior, if one walks under, and through it. It is physical, yet it is also an interior, in this case, however, of the mind.

'Crowds, doubtless, are always unconscious, but this very unconsciousness is perhaps one of the secrets of their strength. In the natural world beings exclusively governed by instinct accomplish acts whose marvellous complexity astounds us. Reason is an attribute of humanity of too recent date and still too imperfect to reveal to us the laws of the unconscious, and still more to take its place. The part played by

00:49:30

is also a way to gather information. Is that media? If people stop to walk in the forest, they often have no clue about the flora and fauna surrounding them. Or biodiversity. How are humans supposed to talk about biodiversity if they are unable to distinguish between a rabbit and a hare? Or even between a hedgehog and a fox? When I've walked through the Amazon, I was never able to control my surroundings. In the city, we seem to be able to control everything. We seem to, and we believe we are. But just who is controlling it? Who is in charge? Earlier it was a president or a mayor, but now who is in charge? The modern human being is free; at least that is what he thinks. And this is why we must also speak about interiority. The idea of an exterior is a strange one, because humans are only able to perceive interiors. The forest canopy is an interior, if one walks under, and through it. It is physical, yet it is also an interior; in this case, however, of the mind.

'Crowds, doubtless, are always unconscious, but this very unconsciousness is perhaps one of the secrets of their strength. In the natural world beings exclusively governed by instinct accomplish acts whose marvellous complexity astounds us. Reason is an attribute of humanity of too recent date and still too imperfect to reveal to us the laws of the unconscious, and still more to take its place. The part played by

the unconscious in all our acts is immense, and that played by reason very small. The unconscious acts like a force still unknown.

If we wish, then, to remain within the narrow but safe limits within which science can attain to knowledge, and not to wander in the domain of vague conjecture and vain hypothesis, all we must do is simply to take note of such phenomena as are accessible to us, and confine ourselves to their consideration. Every conclusion drawn from our observation is, as a rule, premature, for behind the phenomena which we see clearly are other phenomena that we see indistinctly, and perhaps behind these latter, yet others which we do not see at all.'

—Gustave Le Bon, *The Crowd: A Study of the Popular Mind* (New York: Macmillan Co., 1896).

00:54:00

00:58:30

01:00:45

01:03:00

01:09:45

山海 畑の幸と鴨肉 それに太い
うどんを煮込んで召し上って頂きます

01:12:00

山海畑の幸を鴨肉それに太い

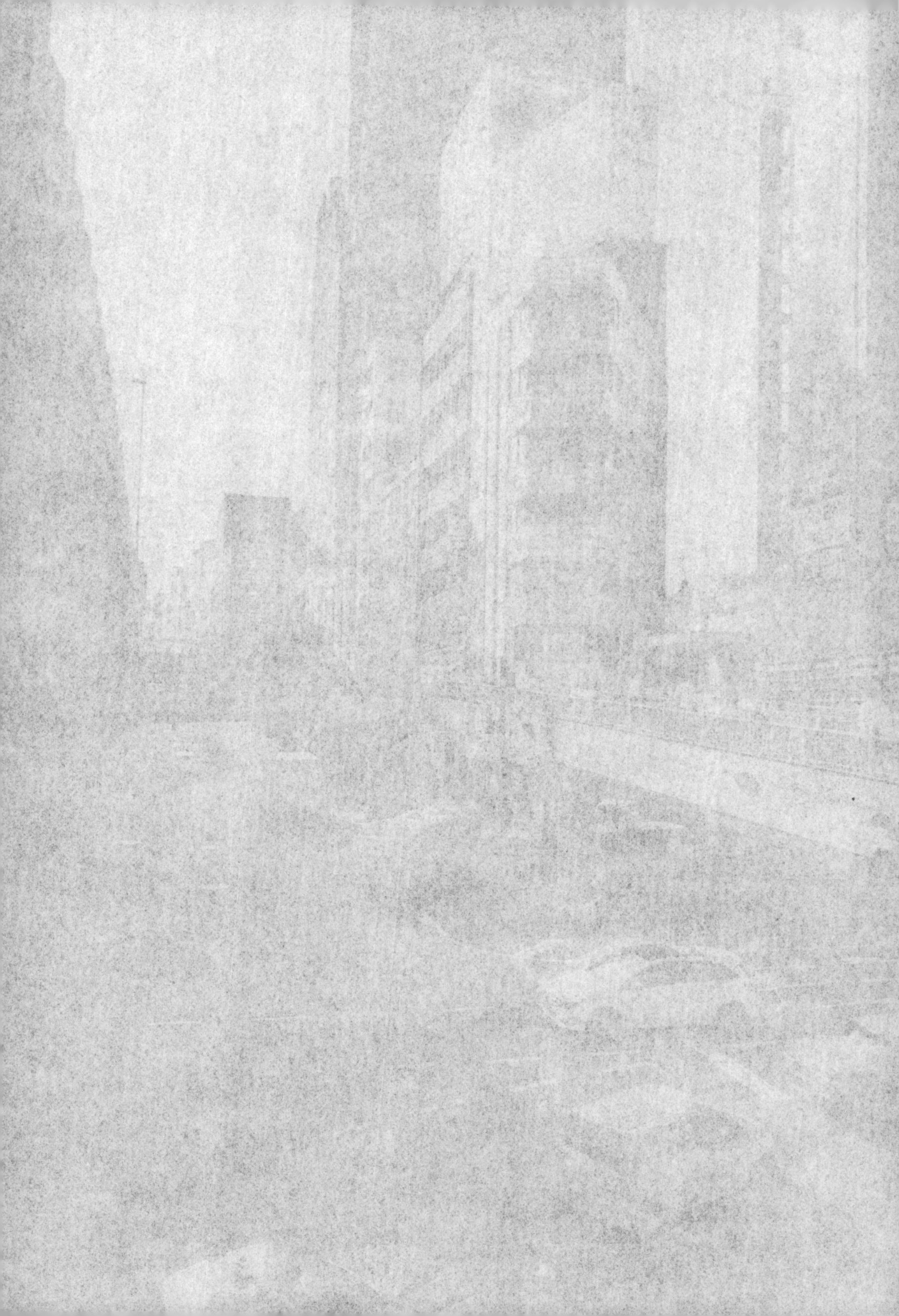

GMOクリック証券
Y-SAPIX
宮地楽器
音楽教室
難関大学
現役合格塾
Y-SAPIX
渋谷校
中学生コース
高校生コース
もみほぐし
アットスタイル
マンツーマン英会話
イングリッシュ・ビレッジ
アコム
5F
げんき薬局
薬
薬
本経済大学
大学院
DVD鑑賞
docomo
como
DyDo

01:12:00 —
02:24:00

COUNTRYSIDE

WHERE THE CITY STOPS THE COUNTRYSIDE BEGINS.

01:12:00 —
02:24:00

COUNTRYSIDE

WHERE THE CITY
STOPS THE COUNTRY-
SIDE BEGINS.

PROMPTER

Let's speak about the relationship between man and nature; the influence of man on nature is immense. In fact, it's so immense that one could say nature no longer works without man. The idea that we, as humans, live in the city and that outside of these cities there is only countryside, remains only as a romantic notion. Nature no longer works without us. If we don't care for, maintain, or rethink the activities we've already started that disrupt true nature, such as nuclear power and the chemical industry; if we were endlessly absent from our world, what we call nature might not be able to survive. It seems to be an interesting idea for architects to think about the relation between these antipodes: humans, the city, and nature.

THE ARCHITECT

There are two issues to distinguish. One is that there will be splits between the city, the megapolis, and the countryside, because we should understand that living in a city is not necessarily a negative situation to find one's self in, in comparison with inhabiting the industrial cities of the nineteenth century. Today many cities, because of technological improvements, are a much more pleasant place to be, and I believe that this has to do with human beings understanding programmatic issues. We don't like to travel too much during our daily routines. So, within a maximum commuting distance of seventy-two minutes – for instance, from home to work – most people want to define all the programmatic demands that constitute their lives. But within this radius we also find public spaces and parks – like Central Park in Manhattan, for instance. Architecture, as an act of urban making, should provide to us a certain quality: outdoor space, a private, public, and semi-public feeling, combined with technical amenities. Architecture should have heating and cooling; though climatic and acoustic features that belong to modern buildings. And so we have to develop a strategy for the city in which

ninety-five per cent of people will say, 'That's where I want to live, work, and play.' Hence living spaces will also be production spaces, and production plants, and to stimulate the body and mind.

One advantage of this will be the development of a system that strives to achieve CO^2 neutral output, and zero energy use, while also producing energy. This means that our cities will consume much less energy. I'm very positive about this. Although we should be honest, and not make use of dirty political games, since by now we know that the iPhone is in fact extremely energy consuming. I believe what we call green energy will be developed within the next century, whatever green may be. I have no clue what will be developed from wind power, or from the sea. I'm not negative about power plants, as in coal or nuclear, for instance, but in the short run, as we all know, the negative of this type of energy is the rubbish that it produces, and we really have no clue how to deal with such waste output. The debate about energy is in everyone's focus, and everyone knows that we have to find a long-term solution. Imagine if we were positive in our outlook; we would be sure that we'd find new solutions. People would then live in cities, and nature could return to its natural state. Although I do agree that humans are selfish and have made a large part of what we currently call nature, but humans have also destroyed it. I spent part of the summer of 2012 in a portion of the Amazon where there are supposedly forty-two tribes in a 24,000 km^2 area, which have never come in contact with modern civilization. I hope that this location in the Amazon – and other places in the world with uncontacted tribes – will soon become forbidden places, alongside parts of the ocean. There should be strategies concerning which parts of the ocean we can use for fishing and for recreational purposes. We should identify areas to return to nature, which we then deem off limits.

I see the world as becoming one big city, with some forbidden areas. At this moment, the leaders of individual nation states, are still able to speak about their respective nations as a whole, as just that – nations. But in the next decades we will have a completely new political system, with completely different types

of world leaders. I'm very positive about the future of the planet Earth, because we understand that our current practices cannot be continued. That artificial nature and the living species must be respected without us intervening. It could be recreation, growing food, anything that depends on nature without destroying or changing it irrevocably. We do this already, because we need to eat, and we are once again eating more and more natural products. I believe, partially, that we will change our eating habits, and perhaps, even begin ingesting pills, of artificial and nutrient-rich foods.

PROMPTER

I expected, from where you started, that you would say we should let nature be nature, and consider food production as being part of the city.

THE ARCHITECT

We need, for now at least, nuclear reactors, and we will continue to need heat. But I also believe that we'll leave all of this behind us eventually, and develop new production plant methods. Although, I'm utterly against the way we use animals. For instance, how we now grow cows and chickens, for food, is terrible. And in the end, if we want meat, it might cost us €1,000 a kilogram. But we must respect animals, and therefore, not need, or want, such meat. Marco Westmaas, for instance, is a chef developing artificial meat in the Netherlands. He's creating artificial food, within an 'artificial' country, which is mostly below sea level, with a near entirely human made landscape. At one of my office's holiday dinners, he served artificial meat and vegetables. The meat tasted like teriyaki; it smelt great, tasted great, but it wasn't real meat. But it was great food. He's a young innovative chef, making artificial foods. We will soon enter a period in which we start to produce energy and food, which we now create from nature, artificially. The ways in which we now produce food are very primitive; little about agriculture has changed in millennia. If you were to ask me: 'How?' I'll tell you that I don't exactly know. But I do know that a large portion of our future food will be produced

of world leaders. I'm very positive about the future of the planet Earth, because we understand that our current practices cannot be continued. That artificial nature and the living species must be respected without us intervening. It could be recreation, growing food, anything that depends on nature without destroying or changing it irrevocably. We do this already, because we need to eat, and we are once again eating more and more natural products. I believe, partially, that we will change our eating habits, and perhaps, even begin ingesting pills, of artificial and nutrient-rich foods.

PROMPTER

I expected, from where you started, that you would say we should let nature be nature, and consider food production as being part of the city.

THE ARCHITECT

We need, for now at least, nuclear reactors, and we will continue to need heat. But I also believe that we'll leave all of this behind us eventually, and develop new production plant methods. Although, I'm utterly against the way we use animals. For instance, how we now grow cows and chickens, for food, is terrible. And in the end, if we want meat, it might cost us €1,000 a kilogram. But we must respect animals, and therefore, not need, or want, such meat. Marco Westmaas, for instance, is a chef developing artificial meat in the Netherlands. He's creating artificial food, within an 'artificial' country, which is mostly below sea level, with a near entirely human made landscape. At one of my office's holiday dinners, he served artificial meat and vegetables. The meat tasted like teriyaki; it smelt great, tasted great, but it wasn't real meat. But it was great food. He's a young innovative chef, making artificial foods. We will soon enter a period in which we start to produce energy and food, which we now create from nature, artificially. The ways in which we now produce food are very primitive; little about agriculture has changed in millennia. If you were to ask me: 'How?' I'll tell you that I don't exactly know. But I do know that a large portion of our future food will be produced

in cities. I don't say that this should be black and white. We should develop strategies to start this process of change within our society. If you compare the nineteenth and twentieth centuries; think about how much the world has changed during these periods. How can we continue this progress over the next century? I believe that new technology, the computer, the robot, and the gradually artificial human being, will one day help us on our forward progression. I'm certain that we will develop completely artificial humans. If, in the future, someone's eye no longer works, perhaps we'll grow them a new one. From natural nature, to the artificial, and everything in between, will be humans' materials palette. And we must understand that character, ethics, and respect will come further into focus during the next generation.

This emerging artificial world will be heavily dependent on technology, which will help us as far as apparatuses are concerned, as well as food, energy, and all the programmatic conditions now heavily dependent on nature. We'll live in harmony with nature, on one hand, but on the other, we will live in harmony with an artificial something. Let's call it a robot capable of autonomous thought. And of course, we are going to use our orbit for production of foods, energy, and holidays. That should be a big fantasy for us. We, as architects, should develop new programs and scenarios for this future potential. How to deal with food, for example? Architects can deal with issues like these, and devise new scenarios. The city will be an artificial entity, which we should understand and anticipate, in a positive way.

'200 years from now, give or take, the robot-people of Earth will look back on the early years of the twenty-first century as the beginning of a remarkable renaissance in art and culture.

01:23:15

That may sound unlikely to many of us in the present. In the past few decades, we've seen how technology has threatened the old order in cultural businesses, including the decimation of the music industry, the death of the cable subscription, the annihilation of newspapers and the laying to waste of independent bookstores. But things are turning around; for people of the future, our time may be remembered as a period not of death, but of rejuvenation and rebirth. Part of the story is in the art itself. In just about every cultural medium, whether movies or music or books or the visual arts, digital technology is letting in new voices, creating new formats for exploration, and allowing fans and other creators to participate in a glorious remixing of the work.

That may sound unlikely to many of us in the present. In the past few decades, we've seen how technology has threatened the old order in cultural businesses, including the decimation of the music industry, the death of the cable subscription, the annihilation of newspapers and the laying to waste of independent bookstores. But things are turning around; for people of the future, our time may be remembered as a period not of death, but of rejuvenation and rebirth. Part of the story is in the art itself. In just about every cultural medium, whether movies or music or books or the visual arts, digital technology is letting in new voices, creating new formats for exploration, and allowing fans and other creators to participate in a glorious remixing of the work.

This isn't new; from blogs to pod casts to YouTube, the last twenty years have been marked by a succession of formats that have led to lower barriers for new and off-the-wall creators.'

—Farhad Manjoo, 'How the Internet Is Saving Culture, Not Killing It', *New York Times*, 15 March, 2017.

PROMPTER

How will our relationship with nature continue to develop in the twenty-first century? When I think of people who live in harmony with nature, they are actually very dependent on it. They worship and respect nature, because all their food, clothes, and building materials, come directly from natural sources. If we are becoming independent of nature, then why should we care about it? If the city is to become a wholesome place, nature could become uninteresting and even cheap. How will we maintain and sustain our relationship to nature? Why do we still need nature if it is no longer, Mother Earth? If nature is no longer present in our daily lives, what will be nature's unconscious role?

THE ARCHITECT

It has to do with respect. Respect and trying to understand one another should be critical to every debate. Multicultural, intercultural, and racial issues will hopefully dissipate by 2085, as the world's population continues to educate itself. The Arab Spring and ongoing Arab Winter, indicate that we have to take everyone, including nature and its animals, quite seriously. There is more power today, and many nations are saying we have to be civilized, all so that we are able to live peacefully together. Sixty years ago, it was only the wealthy that were able to attend university, and now

nearly everyone in Europe is able; state governments have heavily subsidized education on the Continent. And European society continues to become more educated. Learning by mistake; trial and error; history and having an open mindset; being able to learn from one another; these acts are all of great importance to society, today, just as they will be tomorrow. In the West, we keep asking questions; we think about respect and responsibility, but that doesn't mean we won't sometimes make the wrong decision. And the same is true, of course, of the East.

In the future we'll have to have even more respect for one another, and for our planet – Mother Earth. Which is actually an interesting phrase: Mother Earth. Our relationships with our own mothers, fathers, and to our family and friends, has dramatically changed.

We will soon live in a very different symbiosis with Mother Earth, because the human being will become extremely individualistic, while still being part of a group, through our seemingly invisible digital technology. In previous days one had to live as part of a tribe or village, dependent on one as much as the other, and dependent on eco-systems. But as our world becomes much more artificial, human being will live much more as individuals who choose their own friends and social groups, or clubs. What we'll see is that interpersonal relations will change dramatically, as well as the relationship between nature and humans. We will soon, again, become nomadic; it's already happening. One day soon our relationship to our Earth will transform, because we won't depend on it for natural resources that can be replenished. Our world is so artificial already, and the human body will only continue to evolve within this context.

PROMPTER
What do you think about the evolution of our political systems?

THE ARCHITECT
I watch political debates; I see that we all seem to have the same political agenda. Though, we must remember that everyone has

nearly everyone in Europe is able; state governments have heavily subsidized education on the Continent. And European society continues to become more educated. Learning by mistake; trial and error; history and having an open mindset; being able to learn from one another; these acts are all of great importance to society, today. Just as they will be tomorrow. In the West, we keep asking questions; we think about respect and responsibility, but that doesn't means we won't sometimes make the wrong decision. And the same is true, of course, of the East.

In the future we'll have to have even more respect for one another, and for our planet – Mother Earth. Which is actually an interesting phrase: Mother Earth. Our relationships with our own mothers, fathers, and to our family and friends, has dramatically changed.

We will soon live in a very different symbiosis with Mother Earth, because the human being will become extremely individualistic, while still being part of a group, through our seemingly invisible digital technology. In previous days one had to live as part of a tribe or village, dependent on one as much as the other, and dependent on eco-systems. But as our world becomes much more artificial, human being will live much more as individuals who choose their own friends and social groups, or clubs. What we'll see is that interpersonal relations will change dramatically, as well as the relationship between nature and humans. We will soon, again, become nomadic; it's already happening. One day soon our relationship to our Earth will transform, because we won't depend on it for natural resources that can be replenished. Our world is so artificial already, and the human body will only continue to evolve within this context.

PROMPTER

What do you think about the evolution of our political systems?

THE ARCHITECT

I watch political debates; I see that we all seem to have the same political agenda. Though, we must remember that everyone has

their own definition and explanation of the word *agenda*. Agenda differences that stem from the early-twentieth century are over, and we are more or less moving forward. But besides political power, there is also a power of companies and networks, such as Facebook, Apple, and Alphabet, for instance. Such organizations are simply about people. And people tend to live in quite nomadic ways today, as part of more than one family or group. We can certainly be members of more than one club.

PROMPTER

That refers to your statement regarding interpersonal relations, and how they'll change according to the rising importance of digital networking. Could you elaborate?

'This study examined online social networking usage and its impact on relationship quality and psychological adjustment. 541 Canadian undergraduate students completed questionnaires focused on Facebook usage trends and the time spent in online interactions. Students were initially categorized according to their time spend on Facebook and a subset (N=284) completed questionnaires designed to assess offline face to face relationship quality, online

01:32:15

interaction quality and content as well as levels of self-esteem and depression. Results indicated that Facebook usage was not significantly related to psychological adjustment. However, results also suggested a significant positive relationship between friendship quality and self-esteem under conditions of low Facebook usage. Furthermore, results indicate that it may not be the number of hours spent daily on Facebook, but the extent to which relationships are mediated online that predicts psychological adjustment. Relationship maintenance and coping with relationship conflict online significantly and negatively predicted levels of self-esteem.[7]

[7] Jessica Moorman and Anne Bowker, "The University Facebook Experience: The Role of Social Networking on the Quality of Interpersonal Relationships," ASBBS Journal 7 (2011).

THE ARCHITECT

Today we have different socio-economic and political powers functioning simultaneously. Politicians, or the Pope, no longer

01:34:30

interaction quality and content as well as levels of self-esteem and depression. Results indicated that Facebook usage was not significantly related to psychological adjustment. However, results also suggested a significant positive relationship between friendship quality and self-esteem under conditions of low Facebook usage. Furthermore, results indicate that it may not be the number of hours spent daily on Facebook, but the extent to which relationships are mediated online that predicts psychological adjustment. Relationship maintenance and coping with relationship conflict online significantly and negatively predicted levels of self-esteem.'

—Jessica Moorman and Anne Bowker, 'The University Facebook Experience: The Role of Social Networking on the Quality of Interpersonal Relationships', *AABSS Journal* 11 (2011).

THE ARCHITECT

Today we have different socio-economic and political powers functioning simultaneously. Politicians, or the Pope, no longer

single-handedly decide what gets done, because the voice, and subsequently the power, of the world's population continues to become stronger and stronger. Technology is becoming a power, which in a few years will be available for everyone. I believe that, because of this, the formal and the informal society will weave into one another. Suddenly, people in informal societies will be able to develop themselves much more, through digital technologies. And a risk in the next thirty or forty years is: Who will be in control of that?

'[There have been] three revolutions from a historical perspective. The first was in the first millennium BCE, when writing emerged in an oral world. The second was printing in the fifteenth century, with the advent of Gutenberg and the book. It seems to me that our revolution, the digital one, is the third. It's a revolution that rests on the medium/message binary, in other words, on hard/soft. At the "oral stage", the information medium was the human body and the message was oral. The medium later became paper and the message was written, or printed.

01:36:45

And today the medium is hardware and the message is electronic—it's the third revolution.

Each of these revolutions—that of writing, that of printing, and ours—has transformed practically all aspects of society. Each brought about financial changes, industrial changes, new jobs, changes in language, in science, and even in religion. With writing emerged the religion of the book, and Christianity followed Judaism. When printing appeared it was the Protestant Reformation that surfaced in reaction to Catholicism. Each time there was a revolution in almost every field, and today we can also expect a crisis to affect all similar sectors.'

—Hans Ulrich Obrist, 'Michel Servers', *O32c*, Winter 2013/2014, 120.

In China and Africa, rapid development will occur in short time, but who might control this huge development? That's a big challenge for all of us. I don't believe in one world leader, but a large

number of people from different backgrounds who cooperate to see how we do this, or that. And this occurs across nations. In Europe, for example, where nations have been fighting for so long, there are still many political debates, but there is also a kind of collective goal among the EU nations. All of that – back to the countryside and the city – will require architects and urban designers to develop strategies for the city. But we also have to develop strategies for nature. We have to study how we can leave some places completely free from human intervention.

The big debate about climate change: Is it changing? How is it changing? This is interesting, and in fact it is changing. Maybe we can do something; maybe it is because of CO^2; no one knows exactly. But the climate will change and it's constantly evolving. Because of us or not, this change will have a large impact on how we as human beings live on Earth; where we live and how we will live. That's the big picture.

But I'm always simultaneously interested in the smaller picture: how might this affect the apartment we are designing? Or the way we are moving? Will the cup we drink from be the same cup in twenty years? Will we sleep in a bed like we do today? What will our houses look like? How will they be used in the future? We are designing seven or eight houses in my office now, and I believe that the iPhone will become the starting point of these projects. It's becoming the key to enter your house, and you can use it to turn the lights on before you even arrive home. And it will be the device that we pay for things with, and the device to tell us the condition of our human body. It, or a future iteration of it, will one day become the intermediary between the body and the environment that surrounds us. And this is only the beginning of the possibilities such technology enables.

PROMPTER

Recently I attended a lecture by Jakob von Uexkuell, the founder of the Right Livelihood Award, which is also known as the Alternative Nobel Prize. He believes there are three types of

people: optimists—everything will be fine, no matter what; pessimists—everything will go wrong and there's nothing they can do; possibilists—it will all be great in the end. Therefore, what's the role of the architect, concerning technology? Are they an optimist, believing in the technical evolution, or someone who believes in possibility, who is making things possible?

THE ARCHITECT

Perhaps I don't fit into one of these categorizations, I believe in something else; I believe in progress that's not necessarily reliant on new technology. It can be the opposite. Progressive means that you want to do things better. If you need technology to do that, it's OK. But what is progress? I believe it's simple to define. I believe that in the whole history of mankind, man has never done anything against being progressive. Progressive means that we do things in a better or easier way. Maybe we'll soon discover that we can source energy from ocean waves, and the ocean and its waves will remain—we will not only admire them from a beach. Maybe we will discover a simple tool, a technology that allows us to deal, in an advanced way, with energy from the wind. Is that progressive? Yes. Is it high tech? Maybe not. Progressive, for me, also means the changing of our relationships. Is it change for the better? I don't know. But we have changed our family ties. With Facebook, for example, Marc Zuckerberg didn't start out with the goal of inventing a product; he did something because he wanted to react to, and manipulate, his environment. Is that progress? Is that new?

I was watching a TV program about lover boys. A lover boy is another name for a pimp. Technology now helps these men. Of course that's bad, but it's progress. But then again, progress is not always good. We should fight against what is not good for society, such as sexual slavery. It is the same with medicine, alcohol, and drugs: it may help you, but it's also not so good for your organs. So then, when do you then use it? It's a choice, a choice city. Choice is very important. Optimist, pessimist, possi-

people: optimists – everything will be fine, no matter what; pessimists – everything will go wrong and there's nothing they can do; possibilitists – it will all be great in the end. Therefore, what's the role of the architect, concerning technology? Are they an optimist, believing in the technical evolution, or someone who believes in possibility, who is making things possible?

THE ARCHITECT

Perhaps I don't fit into one of these categorizations. I believe in something else. I believe in progress that's not necessarily reliant on new technology. It can be the opposite. Progressive means that you want to do things better. If you need technology to do that, it's OK. But what is progress? I believe it's simple to define. I believe that in the whole history of mankind, man has never done anything against being progressive. Progressive means that we do things in a better or easier way. Maybe we'll soon discover that we can source energy from ocean waves, and the ocean and its waves will remain – we will not only admire them from a beach. Maybe we will discover a simple tool, a technology that allows us to deal, in an advanced way, with energy from the wind. Is that progressive? Yes. Is it high tech? Maybe not. Progressive, for me, also means the changing of our relationships. Is it change for the better? I don't know. But we have changed our family ties. With Facebook, for example, Marc Zuckerberg didn't start out with the goal of inventing a product; he did something because he wanted to react to, and manipulate, his environment. Is that progress? Is that new?

I was watching a TV program about lover boys. A lover boy is another name for a pimp. Technology now helps these men. Of course that's bad, but it's progress. But then again, progress is not always good. We should fight against what is not good for society, such as sexual slavery. It is the same with medicine, alcohol, and drugs. It may help you, but it's also not so good for your organs. So then, when do you then use it? It's a choice, a choice city. Choice is very important. Optimist; pessimist; possi-

bilist. We live in a choice society. Everyone must respect everyone else, regardless of perceivable differences. And when we collectively make these choices – as we did with the atom bomb – we have the power to decide, collectively, not to use it. It has to do with responsibility, and with choices. Choice is very important. The more developed we are, the more we can consciously make decisions. But first we have to define where and what decisions are based upon, since some will have a global impact. At the same time, I believe the unconsciousness is becoming more prominent. People now say: In a few years books will disappear. The iPad will become hugely successful. It already is. But something, however, will soon replace, and supercede it. But I believe that on some occasions, printed material is much more comfortable, approachable, and easier to relate to. There are two options available. Thus, there are still choices to be made. We all know that the more developed people are – the more intelligence they possess – the more their unconscious develops. I strongly believe that the more one reads, the more one walks in the city; the more one's unconscious is challenged. The opposition between being unconscious and conscious is a debate that human beings must engage in. It is impossible to always walk around consciously; we heavily depend on the unconscious. Knowing that, it's strange that we, as architects and planners, continue to talk as if the only criteria were consciousness.

PROMPTER

If we imagine that only conscious decisions were being made, the world would go in another direction. Take the iPhone: There's a calendar, a phone, but people buy it for reasons that go beyond these basic features that it possesses. With the iPhone, you feel as if you have everything at your fingertips – but you don't. What are your concerns about technology?

THE ARCHITECT

There are certainly concerns. I'm not someone who is interested in all kinds of technological development. All my life I've been

interested in technology, and most of what I read on the subject does trigger my thoughts. And there are currently more products being developed than we could ever even use. The number of products in the world that we actually use only constitutes a small percentage of what actually exists. There are books showcasing ideas and products, but we ride a bike that was, for the most part, in the nineteenth century, with two wheels. Cars haven't changed so much either, since they were invented.

Our glasses are made of different materials; their styles might have changed over the years, but a pair of glasses is still a pair of glasses. But then again, how long have humans been wearing corrective glasses?

Even the houses we've lived in for 5,000 years, have hardly changed. Their basic structure, that is; internally, they're drastically different from those of early Mesopotamia. Mies van der Rohe once said, and I like this quote very much: 'There are only thirty generations between Christ and us.'

PROMPTER

Let's come back to the city. The city and choice; the unconscious and choice. The power plants that Germany shut down in 2012 and 2013, from one day to the next, prove that unconsciousness has huge effects on society as a whole. No matter how much I like the idea of evolution, that we are evolving, I see the unconsciousness as a barrier to evolution. Unconscious decisions do not always lead to good outcomes. Germany took a huge risk by closing its nuclear power plants. But take fishing; people still fish, even though fish stocks are depleting. Yet, people keep fishing.

THE ARCHITECT

Evolution is not a straight line.

PROMPTER

If we compare this to the human body, evolution occurs in two ways: by mutation, which means that a big change remains and continues if it proves to be useful, but dies and won't go on if it's a change toward the bad. The other, is the way of small changes. Could we say that in evolution, the mutations are the unconscious decisions that happen randomly, and the other is the conscious decision?

THE ARCHITECT

I believe that people, and all living creatures, will advance very slowly due to forces within the natural system, and forces from outside that system. The toilet brought us hygiene. And hygiene has had more influence on the development of humans than all other medicinal development. Whereas in ancient Egypt people became forty years old, with hygienic advances, they eventually lived to be sixty, and all because of advancing hygiene. Don't forget that the houses we live in, with heating and natural air, have allowed the body to change over time. As has the food and water we drink. And the act of exercise provides us with a few years of extended life, and all of that together now enables us to live for about eighty-five years. Hygiene alone gave us twenty extra years; it was the biggest step. Our bodies are something we have to be conscious of. The everyday is conscious. Although we must be as humans, we mainly live in an unconscious condition. These aspects of life are interesting to me: the direct and indirect death numbers from natural disasters. The decisions we make have a particular result, but sometimes something happens which nobody ever thought of, and it can have crescendoing effects.

'We don't know enough about low-dose radiation risk: The longterm risks to health of low levels of

radiation are still poorly known, says David J. Brenner. A combination of more studies of exposed populations and basic research is needed.'

—David J. Brenner, 'We Don't Know Enough About Low-Dose Radiation Risk', *Nature*, 5 April, 2011.

THE ARCHITECT

We all have the feeling we are in control. But we're not. We're not as in charge of our issues as much as we think we are. I'm interested in the Unconscious City, because as architects we have, let us say, an influence of ten per cent of our cities, but ten times that much happens which is out of our control. Architects should be more conscious of their effects on the development of our cities. When I teach, it's very rare that I actually tell my students what to do. I try to tell them to be more aware, to think, to have respect, to take responsibility, to be autodidacts themselves, and to push their own reset buttons often. Students should understand that our discipline is much more a strategic discipline, since it is such a slow profession. The normal timeframe for developing a building is about four to eight years. From start to finish, it might be longer. The architectural discipline is so slow, that the impact of other forces on the development of the city, is much bigger. We as architects have to use other forces, other devices.

PROMPTER

Economics obviously have a large influence on the city. One very powerful instrument is the tax law. In Berlin Mitte, over the last few years, it seems that the biggest change has been the development of hotels – there's almost one on every corner. It must be a very powerful mechanism. And it's because banks are willing to lend money to hoteliers. Or, because some

important someone forecasted that Berlin would become an even bigger tourist destination in years in the future. Your thoughts?

THE ARCHITECT

The impact of building the wall separating the East and West had an immediate impact on both sides of Berlin over several decades. We should understand that decisions like this influence everything. The way people live, emotion, and sensation is influenced by the act of building. Even property prices, for example. When we know these issues have a large impact, and when we think about timelines, we should begin to think more strategically. In the mornings, I sit in my bathtub, and look out to the sky for about an hour, and I think. I think about making decisions that make sense. Whether I achieve my goals or not, I do not know, at least until I try.

For example, in the Allianz Headquarters that my office designed in Zürich, we made vertical connections – voids with stairs connecting each floor – that make the building rich, allowing people to communicate in ways not possible within a conventional office building. When I first spoke with the client, I couldn't, for instance, immediately begin to say that this window, with horizontal moving curtains in between the inner and outter glass layer, is better than that one, if such connections were in place. I instead had to explain that the organization will have better results; the people will work better together, with these unexpected connections we'll create. And we did create these connections within that building. In order to do so, I began by talking only about strategic facts. An architect can almost never use architecture as a language when speaking to the client about the issues before them that they have to decide. When I speak with a client for whom my office designs four hundred apartments, I have to explain that if we do it this way, we will achieve that much flexibility. And that, therefore, the apartments would be much more appreciated to live in, and that for the next fifty years people will use the building and reuse it, so that it will have a second and third life. That's a strategy.

PROMPTER

How does this strategy affect the design you do within your office?

THE ARCHITECT

The moment the municipality of Amsterdam asked me to come up with an urban plan for an area of about 3 million m² of usable floor area in Amsterdam South-East, I tried to tell them that I'm going to make a new neighborhood, with dense and equally opposite areas of low density. And that in this area, people can live in houses or apartments, and work in local production plants. And once I've explained the philosophy of the neighborhood that works as a small city, I have to make a strategic plan and show them that what I explained could actually become a reality. We have to present a blueprint, so that everyone can understand the concept. I can't say to them: Look how nice, thick, small, purple, red, comfortable, etc., these buildings are. That doesn't work. I believe that all large gestures in urban development are based on strategic moves. The fact that Manhattan was based on a very rational idea, with one big park at its center, will not change for the next thousand years. Central Park will remain. It was a strategic decision. And a rather successful one, in retrospect.

If one considers the future of Berlin—a city composed of villages, with an abundance of area, extremely dispersed like Los Angeles—it's a completely different outcome than if one would consider the same questions in New York City. And that's because New York City has a limit; at least in the borough of Manhattan. Manhattan, is an island. You can't make it bigger. Maybe Berlin is too big. Here again, I believe in strategic urban decisions. When I speak with a client, such as that of the Allianz Headquarters in Zürich, I have to use strategic device. I can explain about the stairs and voids and organization, and because of that, the total construct of the building with a rhizomatic condition, and the ceiling and façade as a new innovation. To build energy neutral structures is one of the strategic decisions that we, as architects, must take. By doing so, the strategic decisions we do take, will ultimately change architecture radically.

PROMPTER

How does this strategy affect the design you do within your office?

THE ARCHITECT

The moment the municipality of Amsterdam asked me to come up with an urban plan for an area of about 3 million m^2 of usable floor area in Amsterdam South-East, I tried to tell them that I'm going to make a new neighborhood, with dense and equally opposite areas of low density. And that in this area, people can live in houses or apartments, and work in local production plants. And once I've explained the philosophy of the neighborhood that works as a small city, I have to make a strategic plan and show them that what I explained could actually become a reality. We have to present a blueprint, so that everyone can understand the concept. I can't say to them: Look how nice, thick, small, purple, red, comfortable, etc., these buildings are. That doesn't work. I believe that all large gestures in urban development are based on strategic moves. The fact that Manhattan was based on a very rational idea, with one big park at its center, will not change for the next thousand years. Central Park will remain. It was a strategic decision. And a rather successful one, in retrospect.

If one considers the future of Berlin – a city composed of villages, with an abundance of area, extremely dispersed like Los Angeles – it's a completely different outcome than if one would consider the same questions in New York City. And that's because New York City has a limit; at least in the borough of Manhattan. Manhattan, is an island. You can't make it bigger. Maybe Berlin is too big. Here again, I believe in strategic urban decisions. When I speak with a client, such as that of the Allianz Headquarters in Zürich, I have to use strategic device. I can explain about the stairs and voids and organization, and because of that, the total construct of the building with a rhizomatic condition, and the ceiling and façade as a new innovation. To build energy neutral structures is one of the strategic decisions that we, as architects, must take. By doing so, the strategic decisions we do take, will ultimately change architecture radically.

Architecture will no longer be decorum. We will have to think about decisions that matter. Because for the next fifty years, mass is necessary to build zero energy buildings. Because building mass can accommodate cold and heat, it makes temperatures slowly fluctuate. I like such a strategic decision. But the question then is: What is the impact of that decision? What do we see? Here is an example: a decision was taken to reestablish Barcelona's connection to the sea, for the 1992 Summer Olympics; it didn't matter if the buildings were high or too low, for instance. The buildings of the development itself were not the starting point. All of those decisions, regarding each building in the scheme, were of course important, but what was most important was the decision: 'We'll bring the city to the sea.' For Berlin, the important decision would be to say: From now on we will only build zero energy buildings. Imagine if such a decision would be made and we would actually carry it out. It would dramatically change the city. And I believe that in history – regardless of whether one looks to the Egyptians, the Greeks, or the Romans – there will always be traces of strategic ideas that highly impacted cities. And so let us make the 'zero-city' our point of reference.

'Member States are moving ahead with their targets and strategies for low energy buildings. Several Member States have already set up long-term strategies and targets for achieving low energy standards for new houses. For example, in the Netherlands there is a voluntary agreement with industry to reduce energy consumption compared

to the present building codes by twenty-five per cent in 2011 and fifty per cent in 2015 (which is close to passive house) and to have energy neutral buildings in 2020. In the UK the ambition is to have zero carbon homes by 2016. In France by 2012 all new buildings should comply with "low-consumption" standard, and by 2020 be energy positive, i.e. produce energy. Also several regions and municipalities (e.g. in Italy) are moving ahead. Outside Europe, similar developments can be observed with e.g. Japan currently discussing plans to adopt a goal for zero energy buildings by 2030 and some US states such as California.'

—European Commission, 'Low Energy Buildings in Europe: Current State of Play, Definitions and Best Practices,' 25 September, 2009

PROMPTER
Do these strategic decisions influence the way the Unconscious City will be experienced?

03:10:20

to the present building codes by twenty-five per cent in 2011 and fifty per cent in 2015 (which is close to passive house) and to have energy neutral buildings in 2020. In the UK the ambition is to have zero carbon homes by 2016. In France by 2012 all new buildings should comply with “low-consumption” standard, and by 2020 be energy positive, i.e. produce energy. Also several regions and municipalities (e.g. in Italy) are moving ahead. Outside Europe, similar developments can be observed with e.g. Japan currently discussing plans to adopt a goal for zero energy buildings by 2030 and some US states such as California.’

—European Commission, ‘Low Energy Buildings in Europe: Current State of Play, Definitions, and Best Practices’, 25 September, 2009.

PROMPTER
Do these strategic decisions influence the way the Unconscious City will be experienced?

02:01:30

THE ARCHITECT

The fact that we are talking about the Unconscious City – and I do believe that the unconscious has an incredible impact on our cities – doesn't say anything about what cities may look like. The only importance is that we be aware that there exist unconscious forces and conscious forces. The unconscious force in Egypt was, maybe, that the Pharaoh held a belief, and then he built his wishes according to that belief. The unconscious force of the Renaissance was that the human being was placed at the center of everything; humans began to mirror nature. We have to understand that these two forces, the unconscious and conscious, have a balance. And so the interesting question for me is: What, in our time, is the strategic decision that will make a city change and develop? Develop new buildings; make a new kind of library; make a new apparatus, like the iPhone. But also what comes after it; will we one day soon be equipped with wearable technology, even computers, which work in tandem with our own biological systems – as our memory and immune systems? I am incredibly interested in technology, but not technology in general. I'm only interested in technology if it has an impact on the way we make decisions and the ways in which we live.

PROMPTER

How does, or how can, technology influence strategies?

THE ARCHITECT

In the sixty years that we have been flying, we haven't started going faster than 950 km/h. But the Concorde went more than Mach 2, before its last flight in 2003. The moment we can fly Mach 4, and accept that we can shoot a plane into orbit and then slowly bring it out of orbit, we will understand that this method of flying actually saves energy, because we will no longer fly 10,000 km with fuel. Then, one would be able to go to the opera in Sydney tonight, and be back home tomorrow morning. Though at the moment this possibility is limited to a highly privileged portion of society, just as commercial airlines were when they were first introduced in the 1950s, and just as the Concorde was in the

late-1970s, 1980s, 1990s, and early-2000s. Two quick examples: The first man on the Moon gave us the computer. Without the computer this could have never happened. And then the computer became something for everyone. And then, during the first Iraq War, GPS was developed. Many advances in human history, such as the Roman highway or Hitler's *Autobahn*, were actually military developments. Just like the GPS. But what now happens with a GPS? We still drive, yet we now often have no clue where we are. Because we just follow the voice of the GPS. Is that unconscious? So, strategic decisions are devised and followed because of technological inventions, which were historically connected to war, have changed or drastically challenged and changed our world. The landing on the Moon, the computer, the Iraq War, the GPS, and of course virtual reality gaming, because many militaries now train for war on computers, before they even set foot in a war-zone. They were able to utilize this tool. And they were able to have the GPS, because they had satellites. The computer game, the GPS, and the satellites were all connected, allowing for precision bombing. The impact of the GPS is immense.

PROMPTER

One thing we haven't talked about during this conversation is what comes between nature and city: the edge.

THE ARCHITECT

I believe the edge lies at precisely seventy-two minutes.

PROMPTER

That's the extent, right? The seventy-two? When these seventy-two minutes are over, what does that edge look like? The tendency is for people to want to be at the edge. They want their own house and their own garden where their kids can play – at least in the West. But they also want to be within the vicinity of the urban center.

THE ARCHITECT

What you describe is a suburb. And a suburb is often the less expensive place to live. There are some expensive suburbs in cities, where the development suddenly appeared. But in my opinion the big city will be a city with five, six, or even seven city centers. And all of them will have a different identity. That's how I believe the modern city will be. City centers have a certain radius, and I don't say that the edge will be a sharply defined edge. In Tokyo one sees that the Yamanote Line is the edge of city. Everything within that line is within the city. Everything outside of that is a suburb.

PROMPTER

Where will the suburb, then, actually stop?

THE ARCHITECT

There are several edges. One is the edge of city centers. And then there is the edge of the conglomerate of city centers. There are two reasons as to why people choose to live in suburbs: Because it's less expensive, or at least they believe it is, or because there is a fantastic lake or another natural wonder nearby. But then again, that's a different force. I believe that we should leave the countryside unbuilt. We should return it to nature. Suddenly, we have a new world map, where distances between different places are accessed within seventy-two minutes, either by plane, by train, or by foot. I, with the exception of Chicago, live and I work within a seventy-two minute radius, and usually I do that by plane.

PROMPTER

You were speaking about different edges. Is there also an edge at the transition of a suburb and the countryside? Where does the countryside begin?

THE ARCHITECT

The edge will become more specific, and different, also because of new transportation systems. The edge for each city, as Amsterdam, Tokyo, São Paulo, etc., will each have its own character; some are more abrupt, while others are smooth. It will become more three-

dimensional. And three-dimensionality, of course, has its limits. Because, at a certain height, one can no longer breathe. The idea that humans can build skyscrapers of 500 m is interesting, but people won't live in them, but maybe work. One can live in a tower, up to 150 m, or 200 m, max. And this will be the same in a century, because on balconies, at that height, the wind and climate condition do not allow for comfortable living. Within 72 m, there is still a relationship to the ground. And this is important to note. Above that, we can only do so for the next 72 m when we would like to live in an in-between condition. Above 150 m, the apartment, or studio, is for those who enjoy the view, and like to partially live within the clouds.

I strongly believe that within these 72 m, more three-dimensionality for apartments and housing will occur. Above that, of course we can work in offices, and of course we can have production plants, and of course we need leisure. I can easily imagine us landing on top of a 300 m tower, with new types of helicopters and airplanes. I can imagine that everyone will one day be able to fly, and that the outdated airports that are currently being built, outside of cities, will be challenged. I believe that by 2050, at the latest, we will have very different types of airports; they'll be on top of skyscrapers. I truly believe it. And the good thing about all this is that we'll have much closer connections. When arriving at the top of a building, one simply takes the elevator down, and then, there is the city. The movie *Just Imagine*, from 1930, already envisioned and visualized this shared dimensional urban condition, at all dimensions. We should concentrate on the edge of buildings or their façade, and how buildings communicate with one another. What could the spaces between buildings contribute, besides being only a public space. Could it help to generate energy for flying cars and drones? The asphalt on the street and public spaces, but also the façade should be redefined and seen, as the skin of the city.

PROMPTER

This would have drastic consequences for the way we currently use public transportation.

02:10:30

THE ARCHITECT

Our means of transportation will change dramatically in the next decades. Cars will change, public transport systems will change, and airplanes will change. This will have an incredible, revolutionary impact on the development of the city. Imagine what this means for transportation: engines that do not make noise, and emit no pollution. There will be ground-breaking developments and progressions that allow us to quickly traverse shorter distances. We will again be able to hear birds chirping, and we will again open the windows, in order to listen to and enjoy, the sounds of nature. The three-dimensional city will happen in the next twenty or thirty years. And then the limits of cities will be less spread. When we talk about limits, we don't talk about limits in a horizontal way. We talk about limits in a three-dimensional way: the limit to live comfortably is, in my opinion, at the height of 72 m. Of course we can build towers that are 800 m high, but that's something else. It's just not interesting to live 500 m above ground. We can do it, but – and this is exactly what we talked about before – it's a product that is, maybe prestigious, but one that we don't actually need, or have a use for. It's the same with the Burj Khalifa. It's great that it's so high, but why would we build that type of tower everywhere in the world. Why should we build stand alone buildings in the city center?

So, yes, I believe in the edge of cities. With the choices we make, and with the development of new transportation systems, the edge will occur. What we can't predict is where, exactly, that edge will be, but what is clear is that we should limit the sprawl.

02:15:00

02:15:00

02:19:30

02:21:45

02:24:00

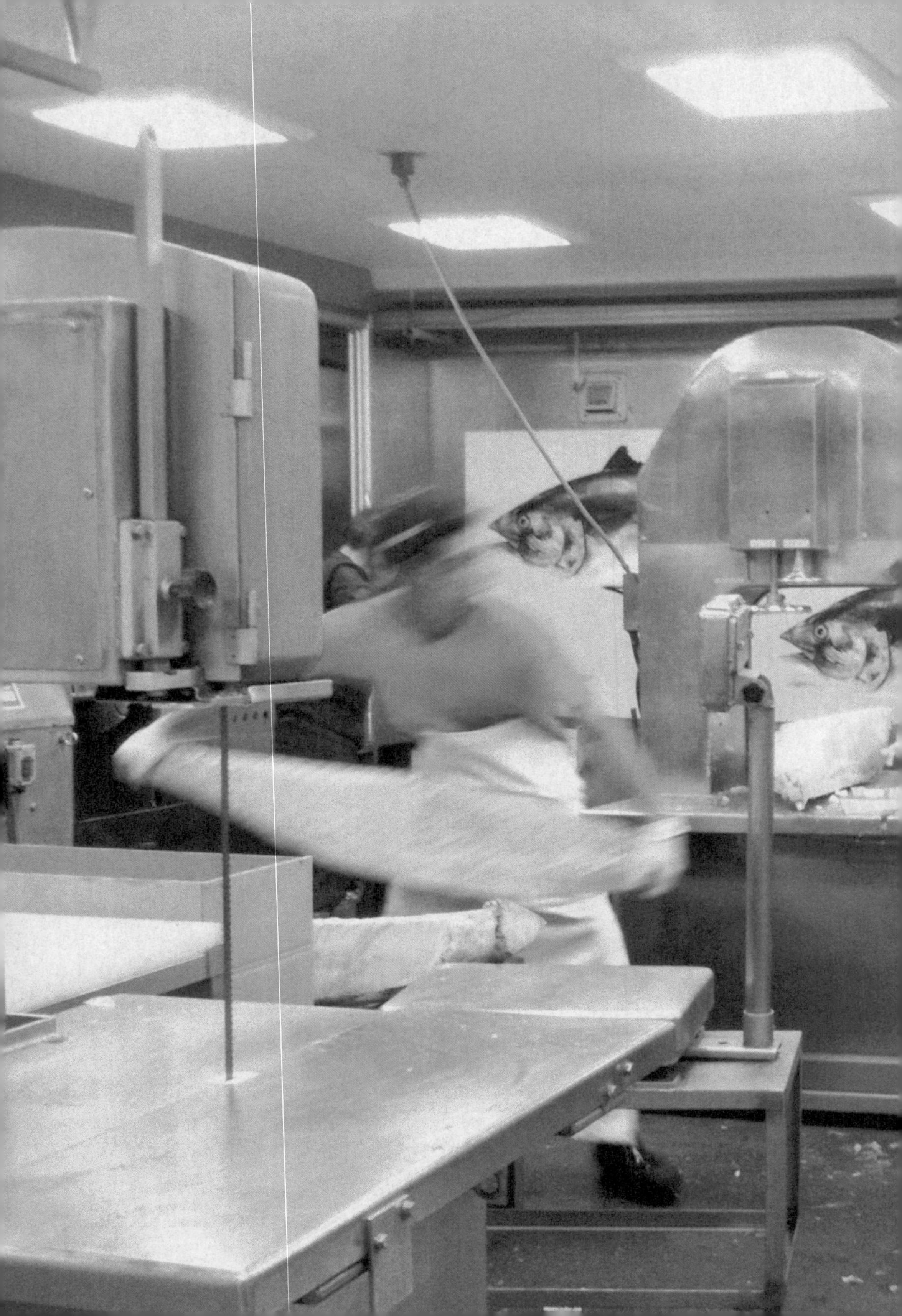

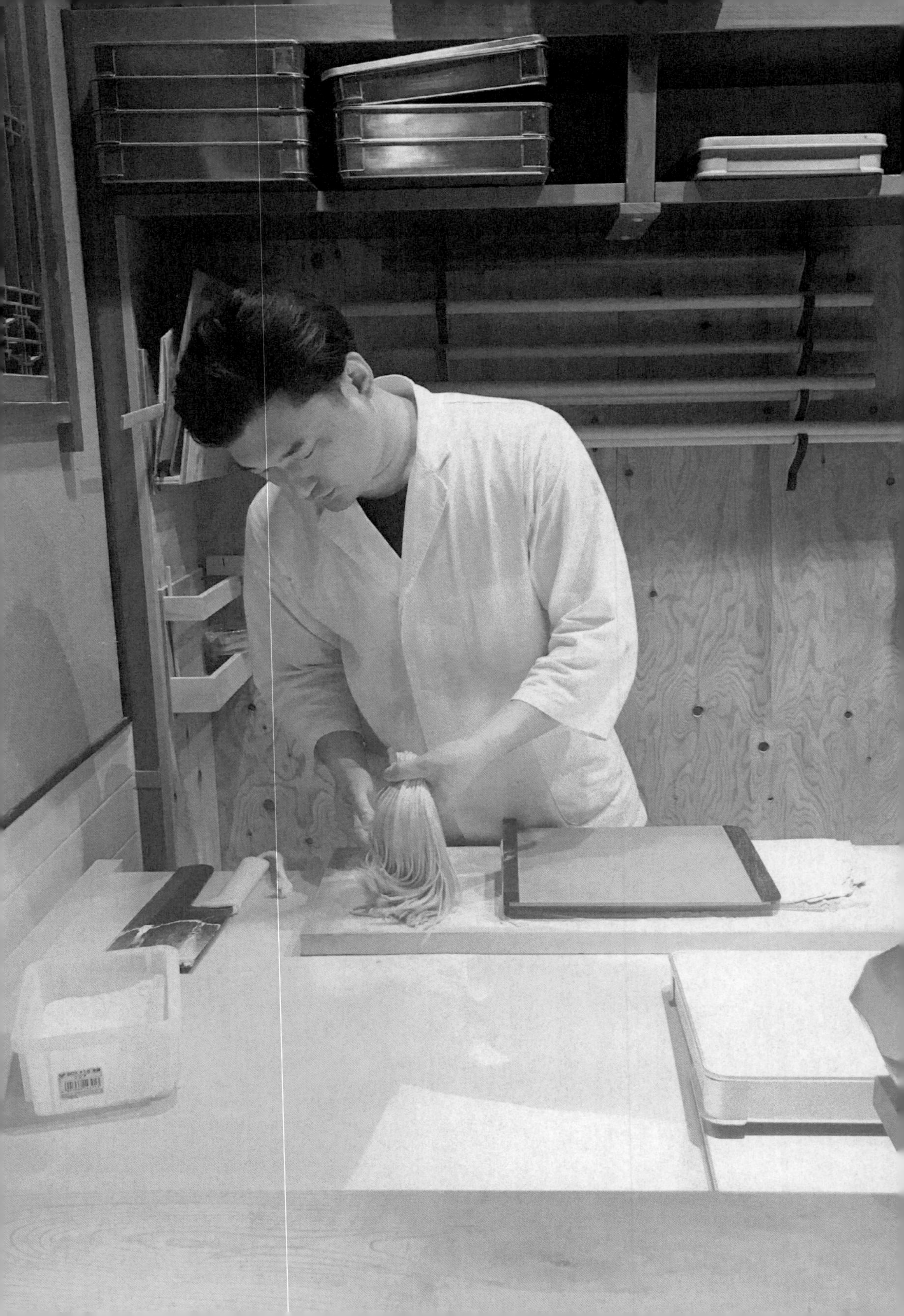

02:24:00 —
03:36:00

ARBEITER

INDIVIDUALS ARE RESPONSIBLE FOR THEIR OWN ACTIONS AND GOVERNMENTS CANNOT BE BLAMED.

02:24:00 —
03:36:00

ARBEITER

INDIVIDUALS
ARE RESPONSIBLE
FOR THEIR OWN
ACTIONS AND
GOVERNMENTS CAN-
NOT BE BLAMED.

02:26:15

PROMPTER

In one of our previous conversations you mentioned Ernst Jünger and his book *Der Arbeiter: Herrschaft und Gestalt*. If someone reading this book had not previously done so, what makes read Ernst Jünger's work worth knowing? Why, to you, is his writing interesting?

THE ARCHITECT

What interests me about *Der Arbeiter*, is that in 1955 Jünger claimed that 'the worker' would, in 2055, be of great importance. He predicted that they, at that time, would occupy the position of a specialist. He foresaw that we would lack specialists, and that people would, more or less, begin to become generalists. According to Jünger, people would work with their brains and no longer with their hands. And so for Jünger, an *Arbeiter* – in 1955 – was someone who had a specialism and was able to produce by their hands, or by means of tools. Either way, they would be able to produce something – to make, create. We already see this happening when we look to countries or areas where everyone is interested in high quality, such as Switzerland or Japan. In these places, it's very rare to find an *Arbeiter*. In these places, for a specialist, you will have to search, and have huge respect for their work. That was something Jünger wrote that intrigued me very much as a student. During that time, I understood that architecture had to do with making, with production, and with knowing your discipline. But now, I'm extremely irritated by generalists, managers, and people who say that they coordinate when they're actually only telling others what to do, without having any knowledge of the discipline.

PROMPTER

How have Jünger's writings influenced the discipline?

THE ARCHITECT

The most interesting aspects of Jünger's writing are his very bold statements, which I consider to have impacted the discipline of architecture. Many architects are now becoming generalists be-

cause of today's technology. And the question is: Is all of this digital technology helping the discipline of architecture? Or hurting it? Today we are so involved with technology, and the computer as a tool does help us to produce, but we no longer make use of models, in the traditional sense. Or, for that matter, most of the tools that architects used when most everything was done by hand. When you draw with a pen, you see that you are drawing and making something, even if it is a line. While drawing, you see that you are drawing. You see the ink being absorbed by the paper. You see the pencil touch the paper. You see the wood being cut, for instance, when you make a model. Everything you did, you saw. And of course you see everything now, too, but in a completely different way. From this digital revolution in architecture, we have learned that materials, and the physical aspect of production during the design process, are very beneficial. We should consider that we are in a parallel space, and that humans, automated technology, and artificial intelligence – as in robots – will produce a portion of the new urban environment we will all soon live within.

When architects still drew or made drawings by hand, they always asked themselves: At what scale am I drawing? They might have thought, 'I'm drawing at 1:100, or 1:50, or 1:1.' But the moment someone sits down and draws with a computer, they stop asking themselves these types of questions. They ask very different questions. They're not physically related to what they're doing, beyond holding a computer's mouse. The medium is there, but the physical relationship between the hand, nose, eyes, fingers, legs, the paper, and the production, is no longer. We now undertake actions, and have no clue, in physical terms, what they lead to. We are unaware of the effects of our own actions.

PROMPTER

Do you see any potential in this disconnection?

THE ARCHITECT

It is both extremely exciting and interesting. But we have to be aware of this large gap, because for a very long time, the architect had a direct physical relationship between the process of de-

signing, the tool he used to simulate, and the product itself. This is no longer the case. And this is happening in many other disciplines as well. Maybe that is why there is a lot of retro oriented decor at the moment, and even a snobbism and longing for stardom. The specialist as the architect has to reset and the discipline has to reinvent itself. When Jünger wrote that text in 1955, just nine years before the first computer in 1964, he would have already understood that we would enter an era in which there is often a disconnection between what one thinks, and what one produces, as a designer. Although he understood the new era to come. That era is currently emerging; one where the worker is, perhaps seemingly more autonomous in their choice of work, and the times at which they work, but even more so at the mercy of the technological networks, which have simultaneously enabled their 'new' lifestyle to manifest. It's an era in which people will have the leisure we now associate with the French aristocracy of the eighteenth century. But that leisure will be at the expense of their privacy, and in some ways, their civil rights.

'How we will spend our time is hard to predict. "He who does not work, neither shall he eat" has been the cornerstone of civilizations through the ages, but that will have vanished. History shows that those who haven't had to work—aristocrats, say—have often spent their time entertaining and developing their artistic and sporting talents while scrupulously

02:33:00

observing elaborate rituals of dress and manners. In this future, creativity is highly valued. We sport ever more fantastic makeup, hairstyles, and clothing. The labor of past ages seems barbaric. But the aristocrats ruled nations; in the AI era, machines are doing all the thinking. Because, over the decades, we've gradually given up our autonomy, step by step, allowing ourselves to be transformed into AI's docile, fabulously pampered pets. As AI whisks us from place to place—visits to family members, art galleries, and musical events—we will look out the windows, as unaware of its plans for us as a poodle on its way to the groomer's.'

—Liu Cixin, 'The Robot Revolution Will Be the Quietest One', *New York Times*, 7 December, 2016.

PROMPTER

In *Der Arbeiter: Herrschaft und Gestalt* what is the relation to time and context?

02:35:15

THE ARCHITECT

World War II was an extremely important moment for Jünger. It changed the position of the worker. Suddenly, there was an abundance of administrative jobs, the white-collar jobs. Everyone wanted to have a job that didn't make their hands dirty. And that was something Jünger was already considering. He stated that this would change our world. Ernst Jünger, who was a soldier on the front in *World War I*, understood that the life of a single soldier was seen as one body in a society that focuses on masses. For me, the reason that cities have changed so drastically from the nineteenth century to the twentieth is because, in the nineteenth, production occurred in the city, and this is no longer the case. In the last few years we've seen that what we previously called science, is now seen as a very conscious act. One works in a given order to get a result, which one then has to prove to make valuable.

PROMPTER

How could this consciousness-based design process further develop? Will the unconscious have a larger influence in the future?

Unconscious Thought Theory and Its Discontents: A Critique of the Critiques, John A. Bargh, Yale University ... There are domains in which conscious processes produce better decisions than unconscious processes, and those in which unconscious processes produce better decisions than conscious processes; it is

02:37:30

THE ARCHITECT

World War II was an extremely important moment for Jünger. It changed the position of the worker. Suddenly, there was an abundance of administrative jobs, the white-collar jobs. Everyone wanted to have a job that didn't make their hands dirty. And that was something Jünger was already considering. He stated that this would change our world. Ernst Jünger, who was a soldier on the front in World War I, understood that the life of a single soldier was seen as one body in a society that focuses on masses. For me, the reason that cities have changed so drastically from the nineteenth century to the twentieth is because, in the nineteenth, production occurred in the city, and this is no longer the case. In the last few years we've seen that what we previously called science, is now seen as a very conscious act. One works in a given order to get a result, which one then has to prove to make valuable.

PROMPTER

How could this consciousness-based design process further develop? Will the unconscious have a larger influence in the future?

Unconscious Thought Theory and Its Discontents: A Critique of the Critiques, John A. Bargh, Yale University'...There are domains in which conscious processes produce better decisions than unconscious processes, and those in which unconscious processes produce better decisions than conscious processes; it is

not a matter of one processing mode being “dumb” and the other one superior in every way. Above all, nearly all higher mental processing is complex enough to be a combination and interaction of conscious and unconscious processes (Dijksterhuis & Aarts, 2010, Shiffrin, 1988), not one or the other in isolation, and so JDM [judgment and decision making] researchers and theorists need to be intellectually open to both...’

—John A. Bargh, ‘Unconscious Thought Theory and its Discontents: A Critique of the Critiques’, *Social Cognition* 29, no. 6 (2011): 629–647.

THE ARCHITECT

In my opinion, the most interesting example of this, in our time, would certainly be Facebook. As a student at Harvard, Marc Zuckerberg, developed Facebook, and even his friends didn’t at first take him seriously. But it all began with an unconscious act. He undertook an action, and suddenly there was the product. And now, of course, almost two billion people around the world use Facebook. Zuckerberg has, since its inception, become extremely wealthy – a billionaire. The question is: Is that development? Either way, it’s fantastic. The Unconscious City is a condition in which things, like Facebook, just happen; where things become feasible in a society that is drastically different from what we have previously known. The Unconscious City does not

even physically exist. It is instead in the minds of all of us. It is a condition by which we perceive our environment. We architects should be aware of this condition. The Unconscious City is a condition in which the local is viewed very differently from how it now appears. Society had a collective memory, and that collective memory we called history. Every individual that has written an entry on Facebook or Twitter has a personal history. And so we could now speak about a collection of individual memories. These also existed in the past, but on a very small scale; travel books from the sixteenth and seventeenth century Europe, being just one such example. Today most of such similar memories, are digital. It is a living history, constantly being rewritten; it is subjective, manipulated view of collective memory. That history had to do with events that occurred on a certain day, at a certain time. But we no longer see the world as we did in the past; we're creating a new history as we speak.

PROMPTER

Is there a relationship between the collective memory and the local? If so, how does it change with different understandings of the local?

THE ARCHITECT

In my opinion our collective memory is dislocated and not currently connected to one particular physical site. But this new collective memory can be used in a progressive way, toward the future. That's a big change. And that is exactly what I promoted when I was dean of the Berlage Institute, with the concept of 'Progressive Research'. We conducted research to create something new, not write reports on what was already known. That method was criticized because research has most dealt with subjects that could be proved. Only with that proof, could one be able to enter the next level. Risk and speculation was not part of that definition of science.

PROMPTER

What else includes, or describes, collective memory?

THE ARCHITECT

An interesting aspect of collective memory is that the world's languages are changing. In the past, European languages were always very formal, and each language had a dictionary, and if you didn't write according to that dictionary, you were an outcast. Language in the Netherlands, language in England, language in Germany was all part of the school of thought that said, 'You have to write like this.' Nowadays, languages are becoming hybrids. Young people no longer care whether you write, for instance, a Dutch word with a 't' or 'd' based on the conjugation – I cite this example because it is a mistake that now occurs quite often in Dutch. People today are even developing their own languages. Is that bad? It was previously seen as bad, in Europe, and still today it's seen as bad if you don't spell words exactly the way they should be. Though next to this, I believe we should still celebrate the specialist. There is a kind of anarchy that has also happened in language, and not only because of laziness. Well, maybe it did happen because of laziness, but a laziness that's now becoming cultivated because people no longer feel the need to belong to traditional collectives. That's because they want to belong to new clubs, new collectives; and the new collective realm that is no longer connected to one particular site or phenomenon. It will be a 'cloud' of memory for humanity. And these clubs have already begun to exist, unconsciously.

PROMPTER

Unconscious. What is it that interests you about this state of mind?

'...Importantly as well, the definition of the unconscious in terms of processing subliminal-strength stimuli was not the original, historic one. In *On*

02:44:15

the *Origin of Species*, Darwin (1859) used the term to refer to "unconscious selection" processes in nature, contrasting them with the intentional and deliberate selection long engaged in by farmers and animal breeders to develop better strains of corn, fatter cows, and woollier sheep. Freud as well (Brill, 1938; Goldsmith, 1934) used the term to refer to behavior and ideation that were not consciously intended or caused—for example, "Freudian slips" and nearly all the examples Freud gives in *The Psychopathology of Everyday Life* (1904) involve unintended behavior, the source or cause of which was unknown to the individual performing the actions (often Freud himself). For both Darwin and Freud, then, the term "unconscious" referred to the

02:46:30

the Origin of Species, Darwin (1859) used the term to refer to "unconscious selection" processes in nature, contrasting them with the intentional and deliberate selection long engaged in by farmers and animal breeders to develop better strains of corn, fatter cows, and woollier sheep. Freud as well (Brill, 1938; Goldsmith, 1934) used the term to refer to behavior and ideation that were not consciously intended or caused-for example, "Freudian slips" and nearly all the examples Freud gives in *The Psychopathology of Everyday Life* (1904) involve unintended behavior, the source or cause of which was unknown to the individual performing the actions (often Freud himself). For both Darwin and Freud, then, the term "unconscious" referred to the

“unintentional” nature of the behavior or process, and the concomitant lack of awareness was not of the stimuli that provoked the behavior but of the influence or consequences of those stimuli (see also Bargh, 1992)...’

—Susan T. Fiske, Daniel T. Gilbert, and Gardner Lindzey, *Handbook of Social Psychology*, Volume 1 (Hoboken: John Wiley & Sons), 290.

THE ARCHITECT

Unconscious. This word is interesting because, throughout the ages, design has stemmed intuitively from it. And this intuition is important. We now create more and more intuitive acts, because a larger group in our society is active within the act of creating. When a small group of people are deemed the creatives, who, then, are the intellectuals? And what is the rest of society doing? In Europe there’s a certain level of economic attainment. And because of that, Europeans are able to pursue many other activities beyond labor. Now, in Europe, more people are able to go to university; meaning it’s no longer important to have a university degree, because you are no longer special because of it, in the way that a person used to be. It is important to distinguish yourself in having a degree; an MA, MSc, MA(Res), or PhD, will make someone a specialist. But only to a certain extent. You should create your own niche; you should become an authority; one has to distinguish himself within the ocean of generalists.

PROMPTER

What then, makes someone special?

THE ARCHITECT

These days, what’s more important than having a degree, is perhaps knowing one’s larger life agenda; what strategy is behind

one's life? There may be many other people interested in similar ideas as yours, with your exact same skills. And this brings with it, the potential to influence one another. We no longer need the laboratory of a major research institute to produce original academic works, as we can now produce it by, perhaps, sitting behind our computer and researching. We need specific research institutes for those who undertake specific research interests. This is why I still strongly believe in language and progressive research. We still have to be precise and challenging, although it is clear that also outside the known trajectory, ideas can begin to flourish.

PROMPTER

Does worldwide connectivity raise the amount of specialists in the world?

THE ARCHITECT

In many informal societies, which comprise about sixty per cent of the world, it's still possible to do things that were not possible before personal computers, the internet, Google, and other community-creating technologies. This instant global connectivity is a very recent phenomenon, and it continues to disseminate information throughout the entire world. But it's only now, that many more people are able to participate in this worldwide exchange of ideas. Many more people are now able to become specialists. When we look back at the uprisings in Libya, Egypt, and Tunisia, the collective unconscious spurred these societies to rise up against their regimes, and because of that, they now have a new collective memory. These people not only wished for change, but also had the knowledge that enabled them to do so. They knew: 'We can do it'. And these uprisings happened because these citizens could contact and connect with one another through social media, through the internet. Geographical borders are no longer. Another outdated border is the idea that one has to be in someone's physical presence to talk to him or her. Now I can talk to millions of people without physically being in their presence. It's now possible to broadcast live to the world, from your phone; but who, if anyone, will be watching what you broadcast? And that shows that the world's old borders are no longer. Of course,

new borders will be created. But it's a completely unstable situation, when one relates it to the society that humans have known for, let's say, the last century.

'...Whatever history will follow, the momentous changes in North Africa remind us that our world is shaped by its cities. The poorer and less democratic parts of the planet have become increasingly urban and that makes change, full of hope and fear, inevitable. That recent uprisings have been assisted by electronic technologies like Facebook and Twitter only reinforces the point that technological change is making cities more, not less, important. Cities aren't just places of economic productivity and cultural innovation. For millennia, they have also been the epicenters of dramatic political upheaval. The Dutch revolt that led to Europe's first modern

republic began in urban Flanders in 1566 with icon-bashing mobs. The American Revolution had roots in the rowdy crowds of Boston, with its Tea Party and its "Boston Massacre", a street fight that left five colonists dead. Urban agitators toppled regimes in Paris in 1789 (and 1830 and 1848), Wuchang in 1911, St. Petersburg in 1917, Leipzig in 1989, and now Tunis in 2011. These uprisings aren't just accidentally urban; they would be unthimkable at low densities. Cities connect agitators, like Sam Adams and John Hancock. Riots require a certain kind of urban congestion; a sea of humanity must overwhelm police power. A protester who engages in some extralegal activity on his own, like throwing a rock at a police officer or solider or yelling out calls to topple a

republic began in urban Flanders in 1566 with icon-bashing mobs. The American Revolution had roots in the rowdy crowds of Boston, with its Tea Party and its “Boston Massacre”, a street fight that left five colonists dead. Urban agitators toppled regimes in Paris in 1789 (and 1830 and 1848), Wuchang in 1911, St. Petersburg in 1917, Leipzig in 1989, and now Tunis in 2011. These uprisings aren’t just accidentally urban; they would be unthinkable at low densities. Cities connect agitators, like Sam Adams and John Hancock. Riots require a certain kind of urban congestion; a sea of humanity must overwhelm police power. A protester who engages in some extralegal activity on his own, like throwing a rock at a police officer or solider or yelling out calls to topple a

dictator, has a pretty good chance of being arrested. The same protester undertaking the same action has almost no chance of being locked up if he is one of thousands...'

—Edward L. Glaser, 'It's Always the Urban Pot That Boils Over', *New York Times*, 1 February, 2011.

PROMPTER

This potential for connectivity is enabling a new collective memory. What impacts will this have on the future development of cities?

THE ARCHITECT

There is a kind of town planning idea, and it's a Western one, which we now see imported to, for instance, Shanghai, or any of the other 'new' cities in Asia that fuse Western and local patterns. This is because, at the moment, there is an incredible economic boom in Asia. Who knows how long it will last; it has recently showed signs of slowing, at least from its height, around the Beijng Olympics. I'm sure that these Asian developments will give way to different mechanisms in the future, creating a different type of city.

Maybe these developments will also happen in Libya and Egypt, because these countries have completely reorganized their societies since 2012. That's also why the unconscious is so important right now. I do not say that the conscious is no longer important. Of course, all basic research, like the development of new medicine; all formal research of this nature will continue to take place. And that's great. But alongside that, I strongly believe that formal research will be influenced, more than ever, by unconscious conditions; that formal research will be stimulated by it.

PROMPTER

With the unconscious occurring more frequently – even if occurring unconsciously – what impact does it have on the notion of 'control'? Is this influence driven by conscious factors?

THE ARCHITECT

I'm very much interested in the uncontrollable. Our time is uncontrollable. Events happen, and we no longer have control of them. Who's in control? That's exactly what happened in the Fukushima nuclear reactor disaster in Japan that occurred in 2012, with the failure of their nuclear reactor, which was only thirty years old. The nuclear reactor is an old fashioned apparatus. And maybe we'll develop a new apparatus tomorrow, or in ten years. Who controls these apparatuses? There's a bank of knowledge, somewhere, but no one has total control of it anymore. We could previously say, 'We'll make a dictionary.' And the thing is, you could see it! Nowadays we put everything in a 'black box', but nobody knows what's in it. You can't push the content button and obtain readout of what's inside. We can't see it anymore; we can no longer touch it. Everything is digital. For me, that's great. It's fantastic. It is part of our new reality.

PROMPTER

Do you enjoy the uncontrollable? Do you control uncontrollable situations?

THE ARCHITECT

I'm very interested in the fact that, every time I fly, when I go to the airport, I sit in a taxi, read a book, and actually, I have no clue where, exactly, I am, when driving between Berlin's Hardenbergstraße (the location of the Berlin University of the Arts) and Tegel Airport. Yet at the end of the ride, the taxi driver says, 'That will be 15 Euro.' Somewhere, between being picked up and my destination, the driver asked me where I was flying to, and I had no immediate clue. I only knew: Tegel Airport – Gate 12. And the guy dropped me off and I sat in the plane and didn't know where I was flying, since I was flying up in the clouds.

That is how my life's schedule is set up. My personal assistant arranges the infrastructure of my schedule for me. I just follow my iPhone. It's so surprising that I've never arrived at the wrong gate, yet. And this is the same with the subway, except there I have to pay a bit more attention; no one is my driver in the subways of the world. I am fascinated by the fact that when sitting in a plane or on a subway, we mostly have no clue as to where we are heading during the trip. We know our destination, but never where we are between our starting point and the final destination; it's a dreamlike state. It's an unconscious act. The subway map of the world intrigues me vastly; it's the future of our world, with all its cities. The world will soon be one large city, with many neighborhoods connected by a transportation system that does not allow us to always know where, exactly, we are doing our traveling.

PROMPTER

Does this mean you see the potential for an uncontrollable state in Tokyo? And if so, why?

THE ARCHITECT

Tokyo is, of course, a construct. Tokyo as we now know it started to appear in 1964. When Tokyo received the honor of hosting the Olympic Games, they decided to build all the highways right through the city. The ground floor is still the public realm, like a carpet, used by the locals very much like streetlife within neighborhoods. The highway system is strung through the city, on what could be called its second, third, and fourth floors. Then they enlarged their city's subway system. And so the physical reality of Tokyo is now simply the idea of 1964's Tokyo. I still think that Tokyo represents the most radical urban plan, because it was implemented through a very democratic process of urban design; they could build whatever, wherever, as long as it's in Tokyo, as long as it's earthquake proof, and as long as it has this envelope, and doesn't block the light of neighbors. It is based on respect. No other city in the world has such progressive building guidelines. But cities in the West will develop these plans in the near future; because of the ways we're using our technology. Strategic progressive urbanism is what I call this.

PROMPTER

You mentioned the city of *and*. What is the impact of the and? And more importantly, what is the *and*?

THE ARCHITECT

Very important! Thanks for bringing this up! The city of the *and*... Le Corbusier's *Vers Une Architecture*; Rossi's *L'Architettura della Città*; and Koolhaas' *Delirious New York*; they all describe their view on what they believe is essential for the metropolis; we know that it will never be one viewpoint which the metropolis is based on. It will always be the one and the other. I believe that we will, actually, utilize the medium of print more in the future, even as the sales of digital books continue to rise. But this doesn't mean the physical book is no longer in demand. It simply means that the physical book, currently, helps the digital book. And vice versa. The amount of books that were printed in editions of more than 10,000 copies was much lower twenty years ago. Now there are hundreds of titles being printed in editions of 10,000 or more. And the reason for this is because there are a much greater number of people today who are aware of and interested in obtaining the knowledge gained through such books. Today we live in a world where a large majority of the world's population has obtained a very high level of societal development. But civilization is not the birthright of any one people. Those societies who have obtained such advanced social development increase their possibility of allowing specialists, which obversely makes it more difficult to establish uniqueness within such societies.

'Richard Sennett is a prime observer of society, an American, a pragmatist who takes the nitty gritty of daily life and turns it into a disquisition on morality. His earlier books include

03:04:30

PROMPTER

You mentioned the city of *and*. What is the impact of the and? And more importantly, what is the *and*?

THE ARCHITECT

Very important! Thanks for bringing this up! The city of the *and*... Le Corbusier's *Vers Une Architecture;* Rossi's *L'Architettura della Cittá*; and Koolhaas' *Delirious New York*; they all describe their view on what they believe is essential for the metropolis; we know that it will never be one viewpoint which the metropolis is based on. It will always be the one and the other. I believe that we will, actually, utilize the medium of print more in the future, even as the sales of digital books continue to rise. But this doesn't mean the physical book is no longer in demand. It simply means that the physical book, currently, helps the digital book. And vice versa. The amount of books that were printed in editions of more than 10,000 copies was much lower twenty years ago. Now there are hundreds of titles being printed in editions of 10,000 or more. And the reason for this is because there are a much greater number of people today who are aware of and interested in obtaining the knowledge gained through such books. Today we live in a world where a large majority of the world's population has obtained a very high level of societal development. But civilization is not the birthright of any one people. Those societies who have obtained such advanced social development increase their possibility of allowing specialists, which obversely makes it more difficult to establish uniqueness within such societies.

'Richard Sennett is a prime observer of society, an American, a pragmatist who takes the nitty gritty of daily life and turns it into a disquisition on morality. His earlier books include

The Fall of Public Man, *The Conscience of the Eye,* and *The Corrosion of Character*. Sennett's knowledge and interests range widely over architecture, art, design, literature and the ever-fluctuating social life of cities. The components of the man-made environment enthrall him. He is an enchanting writer with important things to say. ...Such idealistic ways of making flourish most easily in settled social spaces. The quasi-domestic medieval workshop, containing at most a few dozen people, nurtured a tradition of perfectionism, allowing scope to care about the right choice of materials and methods of construction. These idyllic conditions of making were self-consciously recreated in the late-nineteenth century Arts and Crafts workshops and a surpris-

ing number of high-quality individual craft workshops still exist in the UK in 2008. But current economics work against long-term job tenure. Modern "flexible working" discourages pride in craftsmanship.

Pleasure in making comes from innate, necessary rhythms, and often-slow ones. As we know in our own lives there is much more satisfaction in cooking a meal or caring for small children if we are not in a hurry. Doing a job properly takes the time it takes. Sennett argues in a fascinating way that, while we are working, submerged processes of thought and feeling are in progress. Almost without being aware we set ourselves the highest standard, which "requires us to care about the qualities of cloth or the right way to poach fish." Doing our own work

ing number of high-quality individual craft workshops still exist in the UK in 2008. But current economics work against long-term job tenure. Modern “flexible working” discourages pride in craftsmanship.
Pleasure in making comes from innate, necessary rhythms, and often-slow ones. As we know in our own lives there is much more satisfaction in cooking a meal or caring for small children if we are not in a hurry. Doing a job properly takes the time it takes. Sennett argues in a fascinating way that, while we are working, submerged processes of thought and feeling are in progress. Almost without being aware we set ourselves the highest standard, which “requires us to care about the qualities of cloth or the right way to poach fish.” Doing our own work

well enables us to imagine larger categories of “good” in general. This of course was the belief underpinning manual work in many nineteenth century utopian communities. But where is it now that pressure to deliver has diminished the capacity for contemplation? The best craftsmanship relies on a continuing involvement. It can take many years of practice for complex skills of making to become so deeply engrained that they are there, readily available, almost without the craftsmen being conscious of it. An obvious example is the glass-blower, dependent on tried and trusted ways of using tools, organizing body movements, understanding his idiosyncratic raw materials with a depth of involvement so complete the process of making becomes almost

automatic. The same total mastery of technique can apply to music... ballet dancing, writing. But our lives are so fragmented it is becoming rare...'

—Fiona MacCarthy, 'Practice Makes Perfect', *Guardian*, 9 February, 2008.

PROMPTER

Is that the reason you previously stated that it's difficult to find a specialist? Is it more difficult to become a specialist today, than it formerly was?

THE ARCHITECT

In previous days, when one was a specialist one could be a specialist for life. A shoemaker in 1910, for instance, could be sure to continue his profession in the same way for the coming decades. These days, products change gradually. To remain a specialist in most fields requires constant personal development. Today, perhaps one's professional fields are able to shift.

PROMPTER

Could you give an example?

THE ARCHITECT

The best example of this constant shift is what happened to LG and Nokia, the dominant mobile phone producers of the world. They thought that their phones would be produced for the next decades, and they occasionally introduced small upgrades to excite and entice us, like new protective covers, for instance. But these were only cosmetic upgrades. And then, the iPhone arrived. And, in a split second, a product was suddenly introduced that was, at the time, a completely different phone than anyone had ever seen. It was more than a phone, since our ways of communicating have changed, and so the iPhone is a product

of the *and*. Factoring into this equation was that, as Nokia and LG were no longer conceptually innovating their products, Apple surpassed them in almost all areas of their competing businesses.

Conceptual design, strategic design, and progressive design; I'm very interested in these different processes. Strategic means that you define your goals in an open manner, and make things possible by not defining everything. Previously, urban design was seen in terms of master planning. Actions were undertaken, and you then said to yourself: 'This is what I'm going to do. And now I can't change it; not during the process.' But in strategic design, you always make new choices, which are balanced with the creative design process. This is why I'm also interested in phrases such as Choice City, and Club City. We always make a choice, for instance, as to which clubs we will want to belong. We will belong to more than one club, as distances decreases in relevancy in this digital era. We choose what we engage with. In consequence, we make these choices by choosing certain products, which might be associated with specific clubs. We use these tools to help define ourselves.

Progressive design relates to my interest in history, as long as it provides aspects I can learn from; when I'm aware of something, I'm confronted with it. And so I'm extremely interested in progressiveness; in progressive research. As dean of the Berlage Institute progressive research enabled the school to function as a laboratory, and served as the core of the PhD program. We can and should learn from history, as we as architects should learn from many disciplines. I'd also like to discuss concept. I'm interested in this because a concept is something different than an idea. If you have an idea, you can say, 'This is my idea.' Which could be developed into a concept. The impact of conceptual design is potentially far-reaching and includes strategic and progressive design. This is what I wrote about in my 1989 article entitled, 'The Architecture of Freedom'. Having talked about my understanding of the words strategic, concept, and progressiveness, I'd like to talk about the terms precision, and making. Making has a strong relationship with decisions. Once again,

we choose what we engage with. When cutting a stone, for instance, one has to have knowledge about the stone being cut. To make, one has to have knowledge. And training. I therefore strongly believe in the act of rehearsing.

PROMPTER

...And precision?

THE ARCHITECT

The term precision is closely related to the term perfection. Precision and perfection are closed systems. If something is perfect, there's no reason to get involved in it. On the other hand, the imperfect is an open system. That's also why I believe the iPhone is an extremely interesting apparatus. It tries to be a perfect tool. But it's also open to revisions. The fact that you can develop apps for it makes it an open-source system. And that's how cities and urban planning should be, too.

PROMPTER

Does the comparison of the iPhone with the city and urban planning result in the disappearance of hierarchy?

THE ARCHITECT

Society, as we've known it, has always had a hierarchy. In the old days there was a director, and then there was an *Arbeiter*, who worked for the director, and so on. I believe, very strongly, that the new *Arbeiter* could be his own boss. The new *Arbeiter* would be an incredibly interesting, clever guy – a specialist who is constantly updating their knowledge. Whether he is a plumber or whether he works on cars, or is a heart surgeon; he or she will have to have very specific knowledge to be an *Arbeiter*. Living in an increasing complicated and diverse world, the *Arbeiter* will only work for him or her self. He or she would, maybe, work for a firm, but also for eleven other firms at the same time. This is not necessarily someone who commits their whole life, forty hours a week, to one firm. The new worker has to be a child, a student, a worker, and a retiree – all at the same time. Having said so, I

believe in hierarchy. Though it will develop in a different condition based on quality, knowledge; so more people will be able to development themselves; although simultaneously, everyone will be held more responsible for their actions, which is not as easy as it may seem to be.

PROMPTER

What is the potential of this shifted linearity of being a child, student, working adult, and retiree, simultaneously?

THE ARCHITECT

We do not live in a linear time. It's no longer the case that: you are a child, then you start studying, then you work, and then you retire. You will be a student, as well as be retired, your whole life. So as Johan Huizinga suggested, Homo Ludens and Homo Faber confront one another in this new world of the *and*. Everyone will be more responsible for their own decisions. What is retiring? It means that you cool down, you think, and you do things that were not previously connected to your daily routine. Maybe you golf, or play cards, or you go to the forest for a walk. But shouldn't you be able to do that when you are ten years old? Why shouldn't one be able to 'work' when they're fourteen years of age? There are so many people now who are ten, twelve, and fourteen years old – and other people of all ages – who make interesting things. People that are between the ages of ten and sixteen make the most interesting apps. They work, within our new world. They are producing a product with their knowledge. The phenomena of being a child, student, worker, and being a retiree simultaneously – no longer demands the hierarchy that we previously knew. The creation of cities, which now separate people according to their social class, for instance, will disappear. In the city to come, this will not be like that at all.

PROMPTER

What does the *Arbeiter* do with the dilemma of the day only having twenty-four hours? Does the *Arbeiter* delegate work? Are they still a worker?

THE ARCHITECT

I believe that the new *Arbeiter* has his own responsibility. Which will not be easy. Yet, that doesn't mean that the worker is not working with others, or even delegating. He is a specialist and enjoys working with other specialists.

PROMPTER

Do you experience a similar progress in your office, while teaching, and in your daily life?

THE ARCHITECT

I see, in my office, people working. Sometimes I find myself asking, 'Why is everyone sitting behind their computers? Why don't they step back more often and ask themselves what other tools they could be using simultaneously. I'm sure this does happen, and that I don't see it because I am not always there, as they are, deliberating and debating amongst one another about the progression of a project. But that's what I keep saying; step back and explain to me in a sketch what exactly you are doing. If they can tell me conceptually, then I know that they are producing great work. I would like – at least in my offices – that everyone is a specialist, in the sense of Alexander von Humboldt, and that they talk to one another, and that they all have their own, complete responsibility.

That's why my office is not hierarchical; it's a very flat organization. Everyone entering the office immediately becomes a director of something. He is immediately in charge of his own work. I believe in the total responsibility of the human being, whether they are architects in my office, or whether they are my children. I believe that in this new world the individual should take a hundred per cent responsibility. My children are growing up with a hundred per cent responsibility and I've always treated them as clever people, no matter if they were six weeks old, or twelve years old. It's the same with my students. I'm a student among my students, I'm a child among my children, and I'm a worker amongst those in my office. But for that, you need knowledge, a lot of respect, and also, maybe, undefined rules.

PROMPTER

Which impact does the growing importance of digital media have in this regard?

THE ARCHITECT

Through this new world of digital media, our responsibility toward one another grows. There is a collective feeling of how to behave, and a self-regulating system within our daily lives. We must respect every single human being, just as we must respect, our natural world, and its animals.

03:27:00

global
Only One の住まい
THEグローバル社

03:31:30

global
Only One の住まい
THEグローバル社

03:36:00 —
04:48:00

INFRA

HOW DO HUMANS PHYSICALLY AND MENTALLY MOVE?

PROMPTER

Tokyo is very flat, a carpet, and low. And yet you've stated that it's the world's most three-dimensional city. In your opinion, is Tokyo low in terms of its monuments; the absence of a hierarchical center; the equality between its different programs; or the three-dimensionality of its structure?

THE ARCHITECT

Tokyo is vast and incredibly low with vast areas of only two or three stories high. It's a low-rise city. And in some areas, like Shinjuku, Shibuya, and Roppongi, there are high-rise areas, which are denser. Snaking highways, some of which are even four layers on top of one another, connect these dense nodes of Tokyo to one another. That's where the city becomes three-dimensional, within those areas. But what is most interesting is that the highways are above ground, and through the city. By elevating them, and not building them on the ground, the city continues underneath. It is a city that above and below has a neighborhood-like public realm, accommodating pedestrians and bikes. The city never stops. And below the highways, there are multi-layered underground trains. Most often in Western cities the street is at ground level, and a highway separates one or two neighborhoods. In Tokyo this is not the case. Tokyo is a metropolis with multiple horizontal continuous layers. Even when its elevated highways and trains wind through neighborhoods, the neighborhood on the ground level always continues. Tokyo's highways do not block its carpet, nor its multiple underground layers.

"With the Olympic games just three months away, excitement in Tokyo is mounting to fever pitch. Special Olympic highways and sports facilities are being

03:40:30

PROMPTER

Tokyo is very flat; a carpet, and low. And yet you've stated that it's the world's most three-dimensional city. In your opinion, is Tokyo low in terms of its monuments; the absence of a hierarchical center; the equality between its different programs; or the three-dimensionality of its structure?

THE ARCHITECT

Tokyo is vast and incredibly low, with vast areas of only two or three stories high. It's a low-rise city. And in some areas, like Shinjuku, Shibuya, and Roppongi, there are high-rise areas, which are denser. Snaking highways, some of which are even four layers on top of one another, connect these dense nodes of Tokyo to one another. That's where the city becomes three-dimensional, within those areas. But what is most interesting is that the highways are above ground, and through the city. By elevating them, and not building them on the ground, the city continues underneath. It is a city that above and below has a neighborhood-like public realm, accommodating pedestrians and bikes. The city never stops. And below the highways, there are multi-layered underground trains. Most often in Western cities the street is at ground level, and a highway separates one or two neighborhoods. In Tokyo this is not the case. Tokyo is a metropolis with multiple horizontal continuous layers. Even when its elevated highways and trains wind through neighborhoods, the neighborhood on the ground level always continues. Tokyo's highways do not block its carpet, nor its multiple underground layers.

'With the Olympic games just three months away, excitement in Tokyo is mounting to fever pitch. Special Olympic highways and sports facilities are being

03:40:30

rushed to completion, Olympic songs are being sung, Olympic cleanup drives are under way and the five-ring Olympic symbol is everywhere in evidence.

Officials of the city voice confidence that the great sports festival will be staged successfully here, but they acknowledge that at this point they are a little nervous.

The fruits of almost two billion dollars of spending for improvements are starting to show. New highways are beginning to alleviate traffic jams. Graceful buildings have arisen from unsightly construction sites.

Attractive plazas and parks are appearing where piles of rubble and Earth stood only recently.'

—Emerson Chapin, 'Olympic Fever Mounts in Tokyo', *New York Times*, 12 July, 1964.

03:42:45

PROMPTER

I was recently in Barcelona, driving quite often by car. The city's ring highway, when below ground, is very interesting in the respect that it could be compared to the Ludwig Hilberseimer's ideas regarding street hierarchy. How does Barcelona's infrastructure principles compare to those of Tokyo? What role did the Olympic Games play in the development of each city?

THE ARCHITECT

Barcelona's highway is underground at the site of the Olympic Games; it allows the city to continue to its waterfront. It was the idea of, 'We will bring Barcelona to the sea', which was a clever device, which still works as a strategy to upgrade the city's public realm. In a lecture that I recently gave, I spoke about the effect of the Olympic Games on both Barcelona and Tokyo. These cities benefited drastically from hosting the Olympic Games; Barcelona in 1992 and Tokyo in 1964. Barcelona discovered that it was an old city with an old structure. That's hard to change. And that's the difference between the two cities: Barcelona was aging at the time, as was Tokyo, yet Tokyo had always built and rebuilt itself. Tokyo is built plot by plot with a clear strategy. A strategy has few precise rules, so that freedom begins to exist. At least in my opinion. Whereas Barcelona was crumbling. I'd compare Tokyo to a carpet, a carpet with constantly changing rules, on which a highway can be built or a house can be rebuilt. Yet Barcelona can't escape its Cerdá grid, while in Tokyo there's no such grid to escape.

PROMPTER

Perhaps the most powerful inputs in regards to urbanism will be strategies and not master 'plans'. Somehow, in terms of infrastructure, these inputs for the Olympics Games were master plans. Or would you call them strategies, as you presented them in your lectures?

THE ARCHITECT

To me, there is a difference. An image, brand, strategy, or icon; these words are all easily confused. This is also true of the words master planning, strategy, and project. When the city of Tokyo decided to have a highway running through it, for me, that's a strategic device. And it's a strategy the city immediately implemented. And so it became a project. A master plan is an urban plan a city makes now, and that they over the next ten or twenty, finalize. It's never truly complete, an urban plan. In such, it is for me, quite old fashioned. In such a process there is no taking of time, or progress, into consideration. A strategy is a concept, where one follows a belief, which is then tested and researched and will always change. A strategy has the capacity to develop and is not fixed by rigid stipulations.

For a project in Amsterdam South-East, my office was asked to develop a 3.2 million m^2 area. The strategy was that the building block might be, say, bigger or smaller; it wouldn't have mattered, as long as a clear boundary exists. Within that boundary we could build up to 250 m high, or we could decide to construct canals, lakes, and villas. But, zooming out, you can see that the strategy was that we create zones, in these zones we define density as a zoning condition. That's a project and that's a strategy. The city could then give any architect a commission to develop within certain rules what they wanted, within this framework. We only presume an architect will have to first consider a few rules, precise rules, so freedom starts to exist. A strategy has only a few rules. We don't define that all buildings must be built in brick, or with a pitched roof, because that would be master planning.

Master planning. That's not how one runs a company anymore. Architects are not taken seriously when they are told in which materials to build.

PROMPTER

But do you not think that Barcelona's Cerdá grid approaches this stance?

THE ARCHITECT

It's always the same. It was a great idea for the time in which it was developed, though to limit the building block not only in plan but also in height, is what it concerns. Parameters can be different, as long as there are parameters. The Cerdá plan is very dominant. Not to mean that Barcelona isn't interesting. The fewer precise rules and the less dominant the planning, the more interesting a city will be able to develop. New York City is also built on a grid system, however the many zoning laws it entails, have helped that city to adapt over time.

PROMPTER

Do fewer rules also facilitate the ability to shift between private and public conditions? Rules are very often specific to their program; hence private and public uses have different frameworks, which makes a shift more difficult to achieve.

THE ARCHITECT

When we talk about freedom, it's freedom of the mind, but within these freedoms there are rules, and these rules shouldn't hold anyone back. They should instead be there to assist in progressivism and creativity. When we talk about architecture, urban design, literature, film, and society, the internet is seen as a strategy, which is part of the 'free' world, as a framework to provide information to share with others. Public and private use of all information cannot be totally controlled; this relationship has dramatically shifted. The relationship between public and private will dominate urban design, architecture, and design itself for the next decade. Architecture–for me–will mean being able to develop a building in which one can choose between public or private, within a split second. That's a quality that's very hard to achieve.

PROMPTER

Agreed. Here is an example: a house in the city has some public functions within its backyard, and people move through these public

functions, through a sort of 'hallway', in order to access the private space. Berlin is similar, as it has these public functions that can be wandered through: the yard, the hallway, and the staircase. Berlin has all the urban fabric of a typical nineteenth century city. How does that compare with Tokyo, as Tokyo has different layers?

THE ARCHITECT

Tokyo is a city, and a culture, that is very different from Berlin. There is Japan, and there is the rest of the world. Roland Barthes wrote about these differences in his book, *The Empire of Signs*, published in 1970. Throughout the world people cut their meat, but in Japan they only touch it when they eat it. A chef might cut it, but at the table they touch it, not cut. In the West, we are rough, we shake hands, we cut meat, etc. In Tokyo, borders have a very different meaning from those of the West. People in Tokyo can switch from one condition to another, instantly. That's because in Japan there exists the idea that, for instance, someone is your boss during the day, but at 21:00 he can switch modes, and suddenly he is an equal. Borders change capriciously. Yet the West does not, at least currently, work this way.

PROMPTER

So there are less physical borders, and more invisible ones. How are these invisible borders defined?

THE ARCHITECT

It's a mental condition, it's based on respect, and it's much more modern. Much more subtle. Like changing gears, conditions change. That's why I like Japan so much. Japanese houses are sometimes built 80 cm away from one another, with rice paper between them. Where is the privacy between neighbors? Rather than utilizing a literal physical privacy, there is instead a kind of mental privacy in Japan. One hears what one needs to, and one forgets what doesn't need to be heard. That is quite an interesting mental condition. Come to think of it, it is quite the same relationship that

once existed between, for instance, servants and nobility in sixteenth century France. Sei Shonagons wrote her initially secret diary in 1052, and she had a well-developed eye and ear, with a sharp tongue and with her intuitive knowledge, she described the rich court culture in the aftermath of Emperor Sadako.

We live in a club society. All of us belong to many different clubs—or groups—and this is a very contemporary phenomenon. In earlier generations, it made a difference if you were, for instance, Catholic, or Protestant; there were many divisions. That's why I believe that religion will change dramatically over the next decades and it will certainly not disappear, but it will have completely new definitions. I could even imagine—and in Japan this is already happening—that it's possible to be a member of many different religious conditions. Not always tied to one, their boundaries shift unconsciously. There is a kind of dogma to all of this, and perhaps we are living in a time in which we are trying to rid ourselves of dogma.

PROMPTER

What do you mean when you use the term modern? Do you mean it in the Classical sense, or the contemporary sense? There is a connotation of modern that's almost historic. Do you consider the Unconscious City as a city belonging to a modern state of mind? Or is it more the contemporary; the most progressive?

THE ARCHITECT

That's a good point for me to define. Of course, modern has a connotation. And modern itself is a philosophical term. But modern in architecture is usually thought to mean the International Style of the mid-twentieth century. And we must change that connotation of this word. I don't know what a better word could be. But we must find it. Nowadays there's a minority of people are able to think how I would like to see people think. There's a minority who think progressively. I call this modern, for no other reason than that I don't have a better word. Perhaps *newness* is the word I

03:54:00

once existed between, for instance, servants and nobility, in sixteenth century France. Sei Shōnagons wrote her, initially secret diary in 1052, and she had a well-developed eye and ear, with a sharp tongue and with her intuitive knowledge, she described the rich court culture in the aftermath of Emperor Sadako.

We live in a club society. All of us belong to many different clubs – or groups – and this is a very contemporary phenomenon. In earlier generations, it made a difference if you were, for instance, Catholic, or Protestant; there were many divisions. That's why I believe that religion will change dramatically over the next decades and it will certainly not disappear, but it will have completely new definitions. I could even imagine – and in Japan this is already happening – that it's possible to be a member of many different religious conditions. Not always tied to one; their boundaries shift, unconsciously. There is a kind of dogma to all of this, and perhaps we are living in a time in which we are trying to rid ourselves of dogma.

PROMPTER

What do you mean when you use the term modern? Do you mean it in the Classical sense, or the contemporary sense? There is a connotation of modern that's almost historic. Do you consider the Unconscious City as a city belonging to a modern state of mind? Or is it more the contemporary; the most progressive?

THE ARCHITECT

That's a good point for me to define. Of course, modern has a connotation. And modern itself is a philosophical term. But modern in architecture is usually thought to mean the International Style of the mid-twentieth century. And we must change that connotation of this word. I don't know what a better word could be. But we must find it. Nowadays there's a minority of people are able to think how I would like to see people think. There's a minority who think progressively. I call this modern, for no other reason than that I don't have a better word. Perhaps *nowness* is the word I

would use today. The Modern Movement was based on an idea from the Italian Renaissance. During the Renaissance the human body became the focus of the world. And before that it was God, or the Pharaoh. And then there was the Modern Movement in Russia, where Communism and Socialism both began, which positioned the human at the center of society. The human being should think about urban design, in which the human being is the focus, not the society, the God, the ruler, or any war driven agenda. That was a big, big move, from Roman architecture, to that of the Italian Renaissance, to that of the Modern Movement. Now we are three steps further. The world has become one big metropolis with many neighborhoods, in which individual humans can code-decode-and-code, when moving from one condition to the next; surfing from one club to another, mostly in a digital mode.

PROMPTER

This leads to interesting questions, which we can probably not answer now, but the reason we're thinking about these questions might already be an indicator for an incredibly interesting time yet to come: How will architecture develop and what's the architect's position? Is it only perception that changes the architecture of the Unconscious City?

THE ARCHITECT

There are two developments. There is the physical development, and, more than ever before, mental development; being and feeling, public and private, and shifting world forces. The word shift is extremely important, in the sense that we are able to shift between different conditions, shift from private to public, for instance.

PROMPTER

Will the Unconscious City influence the future of architecture?

THE ARCHITECT

Imagine that within the Unconscious City we would no longer talk about living rooms, bathrooms, bedrooms, and kitchens. That separation belonged to the Modern Movement, with its working, living, and entertaining areas in different sections of the city. These will merge.

The Japanese house, due to the fact that a family had to live on a limited amount of tatami, would and does still change programmatically from bedroom to dining room to living room. And the Rietveld Schröder House and S. R. Crown Hall by Mies van der Rohe, should be seen in similar respect. I think the modern city, even a modern building, must have a certain programmatic condition in the morning, and something else, something very different, in the evening. The changing of program, and the changing of gears; this is what society will work on in the next thirty years. This will change the development of cities and their architecture. It will dramatically change the ways in which we live.

PROMPTER

How will this influence our infrastructure? Will it potentially lower or strengthen the importance of infrastructure?

THE ARCHITECT

Here is a 'for instance'. History has shown that after the introduction of digital tablets, the general assumption was that there would be a reduction of printed matter. And we now know that this is not true. The introduction of the tablet only changed what books we decide to print. Another example is the subway. It's going to change how we use our resources; subways will be better equipped in the future, and even easier to use. But it could be that we will, in the future, concentrate above ground. Perhaps we could even soon have flying cars. They'll be everywhere in fifty years, like flies are today. The drone is a recent example. And individual buildings will start to 'talk' to each other; they will strategically work as a neighborhood, also in terms of energy. The moment that technology enables us to drive a vehicle on a GPS

system that's zero energy, with no noise, partly or completely individualized; the driverless car will be part of the driverless city, and the computer will drive the zero-zero city. That's the near future. I hope that in the future the use of trains to get from 'A to B' will only be possible on high-speed trains, when traveling long distances. We will develop new vehicles over the next fifty years. As I mentioned before, I wanted to spend most of my frequent flyer miles on a new flight that KLM was about to soon offer. In a minute and thiry-five seconds, it would have taken me 100 km into orbit, and to Sydney in just four hours. It was canceled because of an accident. I believe – though I'm not sure how this will develop over the next few years – that speed and comfort will dominate most, if not all, technological advances. And that individual buildings will start to talk to each other, and that they will strategically work on a neighborhood – also in terms of energy. Here's another example: trains will, one day, in Europe, link only big cities. Frankfurt to Düsseldorf; Amsterdam to Paris. Big distances. Everything between these cities will become nature again. When I want to go shorter distances, I take my zero energy vehicles. This vehicle is a flying car that can go 200 km/h. I could imagine that our cities have towers 250 m high, and that people fly into them with their flying cars, instead of walking through their ground floor front door. This will happen. The difference between collective and individual vehicles will occur through technology, and it will be directed over the next couple of years. This will change our lives, cities, and behaviors. Imagine arriving in a city from above, flying onto the top of a tower, and then going down. It starts to make our cities very different. It starts to make our cities three-dimensional, because of our different access to them. And it should be noted that these ideas are not dreams; they're real.

PROMPTER

You have mentioned in many of your lectures that today the car is useful for many things, but that also makes it useless for many things. With a car, a group can go on holiday and take five people, or the driver can go alone. Cars

can go short or long distances. Yet there could be different vehicles for different purposes: a flying car for long distances, and a very small car for short distances, for instance. That's how we now perceive the city. It's interrupted. How can public transportation react to this?

THE ARCHITECT

This is exactly why I consider Tokyo to be the only city in which new developments are being tested. Not Dubai but Tokyo, because Tokyo has three-dimensionality and a continuation of its urbanity in the form of a ground floor carpet. Tokyo has the perfect infrastructural condition. I'm a very bad public transportation user; I don't use it in most cities. In Tokyo, I use public transportation, alongside the car, taxi, and my bike. I use it there because it's more convenient for vast distances. Comfort should be the reason to choose an infrastructural element. Comfort often directs our choices. Today we still make trains based on nineteenth century models, and on them there's no comfort. If this will always be the case, people won't want to use them. Japan builds on tradition but at the same time is extremely challenging of new technology. The bullet train – Shinkansen – already existed there in 1964. Physical movement occurs with vehicles. It is what we were just talking about and includes aspects such as efficiency or comfort. I'm not a member of a political party who wants to save the world. Be honest and transparent. These arguments for me are nonsense. If you want to save the world and want people to stop using coal for energy, you have to develop better arguments, and develop alternatives.

PROMPTER

What prevents places other than Japan from thinking so progressively?

THE ARCHITECT

I recently heard on the radio that Nokia has made about 600 types of phones. Yet there's only one iPhone, and you can customize it, which makes the number of phones produced by Apple

unaccountably infinite. I board planes with my iPhone. I can pay for things with my iPhone. Will all cities one day have WiFi? What will be the next WiFi?

Let me for once be a bit serious about a negative trend: fear. It sometimes prevents us from thinking and acting progressively. We live in a time where people tell you and I about political differences, and that because of our waste of energy the world will be affected by global warming, the price of fuel will rise, etc... I don't like fear. I don't like the fact that we base movies on fear and political arguments. I think you can only say: This is not the most efficient way to do this; in this way you pollute. I believe in alternatives, in providing choice. In our time, our society; is it not best to be described by decadency, in many aspects; consider our dirty bodies and our dirty minds, polluting cruise ships; dirty food; and all the waste, in the broadest meaning of the word. We are losing much time and personal energy, on arguments that are senseless and useless. And I hope that in my lectures and teaching, I communicate that borders, religion, and race all allow us to make use of the positive. To do so, sometimes we have to be rude. I'm much more interested in a fair society, instead of a fear society. I appreciate the traditional and the belief in technology present in Japan. There is respect for one another alongside the progressiveness and rigorousness of its society. Japan was closed for many years until trade relations were established with the Dutch during the early-seventeenth century; they learned from the Dutch about the technological and scientific innovation then happening in Europe. And they became extremely interested in what they learned, which in turn made them radicalize their eagerness for modernization, and in 1854 they opened their country to trade. Japan was willing to change, in order to develop itself through radical technological innovation. In terms of clean progressiveness I think that there will always be scientists and researchers developing new technologies. No one asked anyone to develop the iPhone. But since the technology is now there, people have begun to use it. I'm very positive about the ways in which we will develop new machines. I think we will develop zero emission machines, with zero noise, too. They will be

comfortable and better alternatives to what we now have. I believe that humans are driven by progress. History proves that. In the near future we'll once again hear birds singing in cities, rather than only machinery and the motors of vehicles.

PROMPTER

Is the amount of necessary energy related to its later attraction? I think that the moment we realize how progressive certain innovations really are, that we will have an attraction to them, which might be because they show us something we haven't yet thought about.

THE ARCHITECT

There was an exhibition at MoMA, 'Information Art: Diagramming Microchips', which took place in 1990. There's an accompanying exhibition catalogue, which includes integrated circuits. A circuit is really old fashioned. Lets call it a chip. These are in our phones. This exhibition showed many circuits, all at the same size, positioned in one room. The choice to use one was based upon the circuit that used the lowest amount of energy. And the one that looked the best, I had the feeling, also used the least energy. The circuit builders are called architects. So when the architect of an integrated circuit uses the least amount of energy, and it looks great, well, that's an interesting aspect to ponder.

'The integrated circuit is one of the most sophisticated and influential products of our technological civilization. It is also among our most complex, most powerful, and least expensive devices, and the smallest.

Its invention in 1958 brought about the microelectronics industry, which today is the second largest in the United States. The impact of the integrated circuit has been revolutionary. Not only has it established entirely new standards for mass production that require methods of fabrication and a degree of precision hitherto unknown in the industrial age, but it has lead to the development of many products that did not exist twenty years ago.'

—Cara McCarty, *Information Art: Diagramming Microchips* (New York: Museum of Modern Art, 1990), 4.

As the architect of a building, I must understand the brief and I must develop something which people will, hopefully, find beautiful. Hopefully because of its progressiveness. There are several types of architects, and I think that I belong amongst those who work in such a way. I have to develop a brief, a strategy, a concept, and at the end, there's a product. And in the end, after several resets, it will be a product with a certain shape. It always develops throughout the process. The result should be a product, a building, which one could describe as an architecture of freedom. But then there are architects who begin with the shape.

PROMPTER

Our understanding of beauty is very subjective,

and so is the acceptance of specific shapes. Most important might be its dependency on external influences and the dependency of its current condition, its time. This requires the analysis you spoke about.

THE ARCHITECT

Those who developed the iPhone didn't start with the object. They started with a question: 'We want to make a new apparatus. How can we use technology, which already partially exists, to make this new apparatus?' Ideas concerning beauty change every week, or perhaps every year, and are culturally independent. That is what we call *taste*; tastes are constantly shifting throughout time. A woman that was considered beautiful in the seventeenth century will look very different from a woman that we consider beautiful in the twenty-first. But beauty is not only connected to the body. It also has to do with what we expect something to be, what a human being, an animal, or a flower should be. Rembrandt van Rijn was able to paint himself by the thickness of his paint, impastoed, in order to reveal in paint, the emotional side of the human body and its inner character; at least according to some twentieth century art historians. Beauty is extremely conditional. This is one of the reasons why I'm so interested in so many other disciplines, film, fashion, and art. Such as in the films, of Godard, in the fashion of Comme des Garçons by Rei Kawakubo, and in the work of Robert Mapplethorpe.

Art is a highly conceptual entity. Someone does something and when I look at it, I have no clue what it is. Does my intuition tell me I see something interesting? Can I see anything? I don't always understand art. But I'm interested in discovery. Can I get something out of what I see? That's what I believe art is. When I go to see a work of an artist, I think: 'Wow. That's great'. I know it's him or her, so I think its great. But does that mean it's really great? Or is it the cult of personality that's been built around him, which makes me think it's great? I'm conditioned by others to think that he is a great artist. It's interesting these days, the difference between Eastern and Western media–they give contrast-

ing info. Be aware, there's a mental conditioning, a brainwashing machine at work within society. In the public sphere, we are brainwashed. Do we have time to be private, to push the reset button? Can you really clean your condition in public? That's a basic question one should always ask. I think we can only start to do something new, when we can completely reset. I'm someone who can take certain wisdom from someone from the past, as a starting point for now. Take for instance Jean-Luc Godard's quote, 'Do what you can do, not what you want to do.' Sometimes I can say what I want to do, but then I have to do what I can do. Very interesting. Paul Valéry speaks about the possibility of creating combinations, which he calls freedom, in his *Cahiers*. Something is interesting when it's not dogmatic. When it's possible to make more than one combination, then there is the possibility of freedom, and flexibility. That should be our mindset for the moment.

PROMPTER

The reset button? Is that why humans still need homes?

THE ARCHITECT

That's a very good point. These days, throughout the duration of a twenty-four hour period, everyone goes through a cycle of being a child, a worker, a student, and a retiree. Do you know the Dutch historian Huizinga's, *Homo Ludens*, published in 1938? He was a Dutch cultural historian, who began to play with the primary formative element in human culture. At the end of the day, everyone is alone on Earth. You are at the table alone and you came alone. You are an entity. Intrinsic connections are family, friends, whatever–but you are alone, and this is not negative. In a couple of years, when there's a machine that's able to create, and recreate, we as humans will need to take time for ourselves, and find ways to push our own reset buttons. Wherever this occurs, that will be home. Home for you could be anywhere. It could be a mountain, or a river. However, Homo Ludens and Homo faber are the starting point of the contemporary metropolis.

PROMPTER

This reminds me of your fascination for a word's ability to have multiple meanings. Or even the necessity of inventing words.

THE ARCHITECT

It's important to give definitions to certain words. I'm always interested in words and their relation to project titles. The word resistance is very important to me. So is rough. Its importance derived from a project I completed during my student years.

PROMPTER

Would you say that the meaning of resistance mainly results from context, triggering and defining it?

'Where there is power, there is resistance, and yet, or rather consequently, this resistance is never in a position of exteriority in relation to power.'

—Michel Foucault, *The History of Sexuality: Volume 1, An Introduction* (New York: Random House, 1978), 94-95.

THE ARCHITECT

Until now, I have never given a definition for the word home. It is a condition and not a physical place. You can feel at home in your apartment. Home has to do with feeling safe, and maybe being bored. There is nothing wrong with being bored. Or crying. These are important emotional conditions that enable one to reset. Maybe home is a bus stop, a forest, a meadow, a beach, or a church. Home is a condition where one is alone and can concentrate. An interiority. Home is where we look into our own mirror. Perhaps that's the best definition I can create, for what I call home.

PROMPTER

Thus the reset button could be compared to being awake and dreaming. A sort of lucid dreaming, even. This is what the brain needs: to reset. To be alone with one's self is to work with and contemplate questions. To think. The relationship between the conditions of consciousness, respective dreaming, and the city are quite fascinating. How does the Unconscious City affect dreaming? I also think that the idea of home is present when I'm dreaming; when I'm turned off; when there's no input. It reflects the relationship between the physical, and the mental.

THE ARCHITECT

There are basic moments in history and urban design that are always connected. Like the Modern Movement and Freud, or Egyptian architecture and Pharaohs. It's always: architecture and philosophy. Everything has to do with the psyche. The Olympic Games deal with both the physical and the mental. The Greeks built their society on the issue of the physical and mental. Le Corbusier and the whole of the International Style were leaning heavily on the Greek ideals of sport. When I was at Columbia University in the 1990s, there was an idea of the body, the extended body, the manipulated body, and the changing of the body; just at the time when many movies about the new human being had come into production. The new human being, and the changing of the body, plays a large role in the development of architecture. That's something I very strongly believe in. If we think about how architecture will change, we also have to take into consideration how our bodies will change. We push the reset button in a completely different way than people did a century ago. How are we able, in this dynamic and over-demanding time, to push our own reset buttons? We talk about wellness – the sauna – but is this somewhere we can really reset? Do we think about more things while sitting in saunas? While in Ryōan-ji in Kyoto, how can one think about nothing? Is anyone able to think about

nothing while contemplating in that rock garden, which was built in the fifteenth century?

PROMPTER

You mentioned Tokyo as a place where the physical and mental conditions can be shifted easily according to your experience. To you, Tokyo is a place where these conditions support one another by their coexistence. Where unconsciousness and interiority are omnipresent.

THE ARCHITECT

I have visited Ryoan-ji several times since 1987, during different season. When visiting, women sit and walk on the wooden floor, hovering above the Earth. They intrigue me. Wood, a wooden floor and column, feet, more feet, and stones. Only their bare feet are visible, facing a garden, full of white gravel. There are fifteen stones surrounded by a sea of gravel. And a wall built of earth as its background. And nothing else. People come there and do seemingly nothing, for hours. It's incredible. That's exactly what I talk about; a mental reset ceremony. Japanese understand the necessity of the physical, in order to create the mental. Roland Barthes' *Empire of Signs* is one of the best introductions to understanding the dialogue between Japan and the West. If I begin on page 500 of a Webster's Dictionary, looking for the meaning of a word, it will have at least three other meanings. And if I were to continue this for a couple of months, I would end up having read the entire dictionary, and in fact end with the same word I began with. All words have, one could say, more or less the same meaning. But what happens when one says horse, tree, or cloud? You're naming something you see. You're giving a name to a shape, or an object. But that word is not a meaning. The meaning is the second step; connecting to a feeling or emotion. That's not rational. That's why, when I was a student, I became extremely interested in philosophy; although I soon developed my own preferences and started to learn to open my mind and started to look and read through my eyes. By the way, there's a fantastic song, an LP, by Mark Almond. They are two people, different bands, and they made

nothing while contemplating in that rock garden, which was built in the fifteenth century?

PROMPTER

You mentioned Tokyo as a place where the physical and mental conditions can be shifted easily according to your experience. To you, Tokyo is a place where these conditions support one another by their coexistence. Where unconsciousness and interiority are omnipresent.

THE ARCHITECT

I have visited Ryōan-ji several times since 1987, during different season. When visiting, women sit and walk on the wooden floor; hovering above the Earth. They intrigue me. Wood, a wooden floor and column, feet, more feet, and stones. Only their bare feet are visible, facing a garden, full of white gravel. There are fifteen stones surrounded by a sea of gravel. And a wall built of earth as its background. And nothing else. People come there and do, seemingly nothing, for hours. It's incredible. That's exactly what I talk about: a mental reset ceremony. Japanese understand the necessity of the physical, in order to create the mental. Roland Barthes' *Empire of Signs* is one of the best introductions to understanding the dialogue between Japan and the West. If I begin on page 300 of a Webster's Dictionary, looking for the meaning of a word, it will have at least three other meanings. And if I were to continue this for a couple of months, I would end up having read the entire dictionary, and in fact end with the same word I began with. All words have, one could say, more or less the same meaning. But what happens when one says horse, tree, or cloud? You're naming something you see. You're giving a name to a shape, or an object. But that word is not a meaning. The meaning is the second step, connecting to a feeling or emotion. That's not rational. That's why, when I was a student, I became extremely interested in philosophy; although I soon developed my own preferences and started to learn to open my mind and started to look and read through my eyes. By the way, there's a fantastic song, an LP, by Mark Almond. They are two people, different bands, and they made

an LP called 'The Last & Live'. The longest song is called 'The City'. Another song I quite like is by Tom Waits. It's called 'House Where Nobody Lives'. In it, he asks himself about a house–the mental condition of that particular house.

Marc Almond—The City
Well, I slept last night
in the open
Down by a redwood tree
Yes, I slept last night in
the open
Just to let, just to let, just
to let my soul free
I don't want to know, I don't
want to go,
I don't want to go back into
the city.
It's just a long long long
lonely taxi ride
Going nowhere.
Well, I slept last night
in the open
(It gets so hot in the city)
Down by a redwood tree
(It gets so hot in the city)
Yes, I slept last night

in the open
Just to let, just to let, just to let my soul free.
I don't want to know, I don't want to go,
I don't want to go back into the city.
It's just a long long long lonely taxi ride
Going nowhere.

Tom Waits—House Where Nobody Lives
There's a house on my block
That's abandoned and cold
Folks moved out of it a
Long time ago
And they took all their things
And they never came back
Looks like it's haunted
With the windows all cracked
And everyone call it
The house, the house where
Nobody lives
Once it held laughter

Once it held dreams
Did they throw it away
Did they know what it means
Did someone's heart break
Or did someone do somebody wrong?
Well the paint was all cracked
It was peeled off of the wood
Papers were stacked on the porch
Where I stood
And the weeds had grown up
Just as high as the door
There were birds in the chimney
And an old chest of drawers
Looks like no one will ever
Come back to the
House were nobody lives
Once it held laughter
Once it held dreams
Did they throw it away
Did they know what it means
Did someone's heart break
Or did someone do someone wrong?
So if you find someone
Someone to have, someone to hold
Don't trade it for silver

Don't trade it for gold
I have all of life's treasures
And they are fine and they
are good
They remind me that houses
Are just made of wood
What makes a house grand
Ain't the roof or the doors
If there's love in a house
It's a palace for sure
Without love...
It ain't nothin but a house
A house where nobody lives
Without love it ain't nothin
But a house, a house where
Nobody lives

PROMPTER
It's very conceptual, for an architect, to like songs about cities and houses.

THE ARCHITECT
Yes. But I like the descriptive emotion toward the city and its houses. Houses belong to the city; they have their own lives, and their own stories, which could be talked about. And I like the way that this connection is described through these lyrics. It's similar with quotes or powerful images. In Le Corbusier's book there is a picture of the Parthenon; yet when you carefully read his text, you immediately think: Le Corbusier. Even though the building was constructed on the Acropolis, beginning in 447 BCE.

Don't trade it for gold
I have all of life's treasures
And they are fine and they
are good
They remind me that houses
Are just made of wood
What makes a house grand
Ain't the roof or the doors
If there's love in a house
It's a palace for sure
Without love...
It ain't nothin but a house
A house where nobody lives
Without love it ain't nothin
But a house, a house where
Nobody lives

PROMPTER

It's very conceptual, for an architect, to like songs about cities and houses.

THE ARCHITECT

Yes. But I like the descriptive emotion toward the city and its houses. Houses belong to the city; they have their own lives, and their own stories, which could be talked about. And I like the way that this connection is described through these lyrics. It's similar with quotes or powerful images. In Le Corbusier's book there is a picture of the Parthenon, yet when you carefully read his text, you immediately think: Le Corbusier. Even though the building was constructed on the Acropolis, beginning in 447 BCE.

PROMPTER

His book would even work as a picture book, because it's so strong. It's so descriptive; it almost doesn't need text. It was much easier for Le Corbusier to find pictures, because he was speaking about machines and their forms. We are talking about the inside, the invisible, and the unconscious. The idea.

THE ARCHITECT

During a lecture I gave in the southern portion of the Netherlands, the following questions were raised: 'What should we do?' And, 'We want to become the cultural capital of Europe, but how?' I've written a text called *Zuidstad*, which in English translates to South City. They asked me to do a lecture. I did it and told them what I thought their product is, what their brand is, and who their market could be. They were so enthusiastic about it that they decided to publish the lecture. Recently I learned that Zuidstad is the trigger to redevelop this area and open the borders to Belgium and Germany. There is a new identity to start off with.

We should talk about the city, which only begins with a population of one million and higher. Under that amount, cities are not cities. In a city one needs some sort of anonymity. The moment there is not, it's not a city. Cities are not villages. A city is not where you know, for instance, Ms. Schmidt, and her dog, and her mother, and her best friends. But perhaps for some people, cities are like this, in their neighborhoods. But not overall. Those in cities today do not know all of their neighbors. On the other hand, when one frequently visits a restaurant, we expect the waitress to know us, and to know our name. When I am in a restaurant, I want the waiter to know whom I am, to know what I am comfortable with, which table, and which wine. Yet although I'm sitting there, in the restaurant, in public, I want to be anonymous. That's the condition of sameness, difference, and private and public. I want to be known when I'm entering, but from that moment on, I want to be anonymous.

PROMPTER

So you only want them to know certain things about you? And not to know something about your kids, for instance? When you go to the bakery, you want them to know the bread you usually buy, but not your favorite coffee and the name of your mom. That's for someone else. Is this what you consider clubbing to be?

THE ARCHITECT

Yes. I go to the barber; he knows how to cut my hair, but not the type of wine I like to drink. Although, he probably believes after a while that he does. Then, maybe, it is time for a change.

PROMPTER

Is this the reason why we don't talk to other people in subways?

THE ARCHITECT

That happens for many reasons. It has to do with proximity. We are too close. Distance to others determines in which condition we are. There are other aspects of space and time to consider too. Distance to one another determines in which condition we are. When designing a bar, or a restaurant, the size of the tables determines much. A project I designed has a custom made table for eighteen to twenty students. They will have a different conversation than a table of only four, and that conversation will have a different outcome. When we are in the subway, and I tell you something, the person next to us is suddenly involved. He listens. Even if he is not showing us he can hear, he is involved. It's this condition that makes us not want to talk when riding subways. And the fact that the elevator, bus, and train all have a short travel time duration. But the proximity in the subways—where people sitting next to one another feel as if they will remain strangers forever—misses the tension arising when sitting next to someone in the airplane. This may have something to do, possibly, with the fact that in the subway, one can always leave at the next stop.

04:34:30

PROMPTER

So you only want them to know certain things about you? And not to know something about your kids, for instance? When you go to the bakery, you want them to know the bread you usually buy, but not your favorite coffee and the name of your mom. That's for someone else. Is this what you consider clubbing to be?

THE ARCHITECT

Yes. I go to the barber; he knows how to cut my hair, but not the type of wine I like to drink. Although, he probably believes after a while that he does. Then, maybe, it is time for a change.

PROMPTER

Is this the reason why we don't talk to other people in subways?

THE ARCHITECT

That happens for many reasons. It has to do with proximity. We are too close. Distance to others determines in which condition we are. There are other aspects of space and time to consider too. Distance to one another determines in which condition we are. When designing a bar, or a restaurant, the size of the tables determines much. A project I designed has a custom made table for eighteen to twenty students. They will have a different conversation than a table of only four, and that conversation will have a different outcome. When we are in the subway, and I tell you something, the person next to us is suddenly involved. He listens. Even if he is not showing us he can hear, he is involved. It's this condition that makes us not want to talk when riding subways. And the fact that the elevator, bus, and train all have a short travel time duration. But the proximity in the subways – where people sitting next to one another feel as if they will remain strangers forever – misses the tension arising when sitting next to someone in the airplane. This may have something to do, possibly, with the fact that in the subway, one can always leave at the next stop.

PROMPTER

Yes. I think it has to do with time. Either we start communicating and then we do it for a certain time, or we don't, and that uncertainty makes us uneasy.

THE ARCHITECT

It also relates to being in a bar, where there's the same proximity, and a mixture of alcohol and music. And the time that we spend in a bar seems to be different. This type of atmosphere doesn't usually stop us from communicating. But, in an airplane, why do I only engage in 'yes and no' talk? I don't usually speak on airplanes.

PROMPTER

Perhaps because you're afraid you can't run off if it doesn't go the way you want it to. You're vulnerable.

THE ARCHITECT

In Berlin there's the phenomena: the *Kiez*, or the quarter. Maybe our brains can't deal with something bigger than a quarter; say, Berlin's Mitte neighborhood. People come to Berlin and think: 'I'm going to be all over this city.' But in reality, they aren't. We aren't able to cope with its size. And that's the basis of my seventy-two minute story. Everything that can be reached in this time period belongs to one's home, one's neighborhood. After seventy-two minutes, we just stay in a hotel. We're not going home.

PROMPTER

Is it related to modes of transport? The kind of transport?

THE ARCHITECT

Of course. When you take an airplane, the destination is further away. I believe that airplanes are the most efficient form of travel. Neighborhoods are getting bigger, and the world is getting smaller. That's the whole point of the story from Paul Virilio: the child was carried by the mother, then the child began to walk himself, and then came the horse, then a horse with a wagon, and then an

engine. Our radius became bigger, our neighborhood became larger, and our world became smaller by simplifying connections.

—Jérôme Sans: The sociologist Michel Maffesoli speaks of the development of "neo-tribalism", a desire to regroup, through all the possibilities of long-distance communication. It seems, nonetheless, that we are still dealing with an experience of solitary satisfaction.

—Paul Virilio: I don't believe in a return of tribes and I don't think that a gang is a tribe. As I said in my book *L'Inertie Polaire*, what's on its way is the planet man, the self-sufficient man who, with the help of technology, no longer needs to reach out to others because others come to him. With cyber-sexuality, he doesn't need to make love at his partner's house, love comes to him instantly, like

04:39:00

engine. Our radius became bigger, our neighborhood became larger, and our world became smaller by simplifying connections.

—Jérôme Sans: The sociologist Michel Maffesoli speaks of the development of “neo-tribalism”, a desire to regroup, through all the possibilities of long-distance communication. It seems, nonetheless, that we are still dealing with an experience of solitary satisfaction.

—Paul Virilio: I don’t believe in a return of tribes and I don’t think that a gang is a tribe. As I said in my book *L’Inertie Polaire*, what’s on its way is the planet man, the self-sufficient man who, with the help of technology, no longer needs to reach out to others because others come to him. With cyber-sexuality, he doesn’t need to make love at his partner’s house, love comes to him instantly, like

a fax or a message on the electronic highway. The future lies in cosmic solitude. I picture a weightless individual in a little ergonomic armchair, suspended outside a space capsule, with the Earth below and the interstellar void above. A man with his own gravity, who no longer needs a relationship to society, to those around him, and least of all to a family. Maffesoli's tribalization is a totally outmoded vision; the future lies in an unimaginable solitude—of which play is one element.'

—Paul Virilio and Jérôme Sans, 'Game Of Love & Chance', *Virtually2k* (1995).

PROMPTER

The bigger the radius becomes, the more holes it will have. It doesn't mean that we know everything within a radius. You don't know everything in your radius; you have to choose. You have to club.

THE ARCHITECT

If you interview a hundred people that have read a particular book, you'd soon discover, after talking to them, that it's not the book that determines the content, and instead who you talk

to about the book. It's the reader who defines the story, not the book. Even when we read the same book, with the same information, it's the people reading that create the story they're reading. We see what we are. With a travel time of seventy-two minutes, we only see what we are able to.

to about the book. It's the reader who defines the story, not the book. Even when we read the same book, with the same information, it's the people reading that create the story they're reading. We see what we are. With a travel time of seventy-two minutes, we only see what we are able to.

04:43:30

カネウ
ロ−111〜2
3543-0977

04:48:00

ロ−111〜2
カネウ
増分
3543-0977
6776

レイク

25019
救命講習修了証
練馬 500
890円

04:48:00 –
06:00:00

PROGRAM

A SEQUENCE
OF INSTRUCTIONS.

THE ARCHITECT

I would agree with you that great ideas, like monuments, are shaped by reality in the same way that memory flows through the life of a person. For me, the *now* is very important, since the now is where we consciously and unconsciously make manifest how we read and feel the city. Unconscious City is how we read the landscape of the city, which is different at every single moment. For Aldo Rossi, the city itself is the collective memory of its people, and the memory it is associated with objects and places. For him, great ideas give shape to architecture and landscapes.

PROMPTER

Collective memory. There's a general understanding of the term, in the context of city planning, which Aldo Rossi brought forth. What does this term mean to you? If one understands collective memory as something quite conscious–referring to Rossi's understanding of collective memory in monuments, that one could only read if one knows what the monument stands for–what would this look like in the Unconscious City? What is the monument replaced with in an Unconscious City? And what about those who don't already know what existing monuments mean? I only know the meaning of a small percentage of Berlin's monuments, but I still share a collective feeling about the city, with others.

THE ARCHITECT

I'm not sure if I should say this so bluntly: I'm interested in great ideas. That is why I like the cinematographical experience, since it's the singular individual that defines the reading. It is the flow, the sequence, the emotional and intellectual montage. Eleanor Roosevelt is said to have once said: "Yesterday is history. Tomorrow is a mystery. Today is a gift. That's why it's called the present." That's a quote to live by.

04:52:30

THE ARCHITECT

I would agree with you that great ideas, like monuments, are shaped by reality in the same way that memory flows through the life of a person. For me, *the now* is very important, since the now is where we consciously and unconsciously make manifest how we read and feel the city. Unconscious City is how we read the landscape of the city, which is different, at every single moment. For Aldo Rossi, the city itself is the collective memory of its people, and the memory it is associated with objects and places. For him, great ideas give shape to architecture and landscapes.

PROMPTER

Collective memory. There's a general understanding of the term, in the context of city planning, which Aldo Rossi brought forth. What does this term mean to you? If one understands collective memory as something quite conscious–referring to Rossi's understanding of collective memory in monuments, that one could only read if one knows what the monument stands for – what would this look like in the Unconscious City? What is the monument replaced with in an Unconscious City? And what about those who don't already know what existing monuments mean? I only know the meaning of a small percentage of Berlin's monuments, but I still share a collective feeling about the city, with others.

THE ARCHITECT

I'm not sure if I should say this so bluntly: I'm interested in great ideas. That is why I like the cinematographical experience, since it's the singular individual that defines the reading. It is the flow, the sequence, the emotional and intellectual montage. Eleanor Roosevelt is said to have once said: 'Yesterday is history. Tomorrow is a mystery. Today is a gift. That's why it's called the present.' That's a quote to live by.

‘We face the future fortified with the lessons we have learned from the past. It is today that we must create the world of the future. Spinoza, I think, pointed out that we ourselves can make experience valuable when, by imagination and reason, we turn it into foresight.’

—Eleanor Roosevelt, *Tomorrow is Now* (New York: Harper & Row, 1963), 15.

THE ARCHITECT

When I’m confronted with a monument, I read it as being in the present. I don’t view a monument in the same way most people view the Pantheon, claiming its history as evidence to support its beauty. Rather, I believe in the city of today. I don’t believe in the city of yesterday, or the city of tomorrow. I believe in the Unconscious City.

I live in *the now*. Every human being is aware of reality, he sees with his two eyes, he hears with his own two ears, he smells with his nose, and he combines all those impressions to form what he, or she, calls reality. And that’s where the Unconscious City begins.

We are constantly processing countless combinations of sensory information. If your mental construction of these stimuli relate to, for instance, a monument–that’s fine. But I’m more interested in the moment one is conscious of what one sees, and the short moment later within that unconscious state, again. I believe that humans perceive the world in a rather unconscious way. We don’t walk through a city in a state of constant consciousness. Dreamlike conditions, and states of wonder, are both components of unconsciousness.

PROMPTER

How can we deal with this unconsciousness when making, dreaming of, or even constructing a new city? It's a rare instance that a new city is constructed at once, according to a few guiding principles.

THE ARCHITECT

A collective memory is not only comprised of memories from the past. Collective memory can also entail memories from only a few seconds ago. Collective memory can also be rooted in the present. Collectiveness combines humans, from all over the world. We are in a constant state of communication. And for me, that communication is our collective memory. That's exactly where I believe, at this instant, our collective memory happens. It is no longer connected to our family, our street, our neighbor, our city, or our country. It's connected to the entire world. The recent revolutions throughout the world, for instance, are events that the whole world has to deal with. And so collective memory has a much larger impact now, than it did in the past.

'Collective Consciousness: The term collective consciousness refers to the condition of the subject within the whole of society, and how any given individual comes to view themselves as a part of any given group. The term has specifically been used by social theorists/ psychoanalysts like Durkheim, Althusser, and Jung to explicate

04:57:00

how an autonomous individual comes to identify with a larger group/structure. Definitively, "collective" means "[formed by [a] collection of individual persons or things; constituting a collection; gathered into one; taken as a whole; aggregate, collected" (OED). Likewise, "consciousness", (a term which is slightly more complex to define with the entirety of its implications) signifies "Joint or mutual knowledge", "Internal knowledge or conviction; knowledge as to which one has the testimony within oneself; esp. of one's own innocence, guilt, deficiencies", and "The state or fact of being mentally conscious or aware of anything" (OED).
By combining the two terms, we can surmise that the phrase collective consciousness implies an internal knowing known by all,

or a consciousness shared by a plurality of persons. The easiest way to think of the phrase (even with its extremely loaded historical content) is to regard it as being an idea or proclivity that we all share, whoever specifically "we" might entail. —Although history credits Émile Durkheim with the coinage of the phrase, many other theorists have engaged the notion. Durkheim and Althusser are concerned with the making of the subject as an aggregation of external processes/societal conditions...'

—Anna Piepmeyer, *'Collective Consciousness'*, The Chicago School of Media Theory (2004).

'The collective unconscious—so far as we can say anything about it at all—appears to consist of mythological motifs or primordial images, for which reason the myths of all nations are its real exponents. In fact, the

whole of mythology could be taken as a sort of projection of the collective unconscious... We can therefore study the collective unconscious in two ways, either in mythology or in the analysis of the individual.'

—Carl Gustav Young, Collected Works of C.G. Jung, Volume 8: *Structure & Dynamics of the Psyche* (London: Routledge, 1970).

THE ARCHITECT

Architecture will have a form, in the end. And when designers make a product, they have to create a form for that product, too. Form is the shape; the configuration; the appearance, the performance of a structure, as we recognize it. And when architects create a building, they have to create a form, or envelope, for that building. When humans make a city, which will, over time, take on a particular contour; cities become layers of history. But humans are no longer in control of any of this, anymore. Even architects are not in control of the shapes, or forms, of their buildings–because a multitude of other factors are involved. How do I then approach a building? How do I create a cinematographic condition? How can I make a building neutral, on the one hand, and specific on the other?

It's very rare that buildings have only one program. And buildings aren't often seen from a singular perspective. How can I, as an architect, become a sort of film director, enabling someone to look at a building in an individually determined way, and encourage them to use that building differently because of that? That's a completely different way of approaching the making of buildings, and architecture, than it was a century ago. Then, buildings were meant to be more specific, and there were even building catalogues: hospitals looked like *this*, libraries looked like *this*, and a

house looked like *that*. They tried to make everything into a typological construct, which I don't believe in. Rather, I believe much more in fluidity, where situations can dissolve, and disappear.

In 1955, when Gerrit Rietveld said that, maybe, walls of a building in the future will consist of magnetic fields–the idea of dematerialized architecture was born. Why should we discuss form when discussing architecture? Why should we talk about blurbs and blobs? That's not the world we live in. Blurbs and blobs do not mirror or mimic nature; they are artificial constructs. Oppositely, and interestingly (and increasingly), buildings do not need to look as if they mimic nature, in order to actually do so. Collective memory must be completely reinterpreted. We have to think about these issues in a very different way, because our collective memory changes every day. When a single product is introduced to the world that progresses communication, globally, our collective memory will change. Events like these alter the ways in which we remember human history. It is more than likely that we will acknowledge a collective unconscious. A few years ago my father passed away, and shortly thereafter my mother passed way. I've learned a lot about death during the past years. I've learned that life is instant. Life is fluid. And yet people always treat life as if *this* or *that* will determine the outcome.

There is a physical aspect to being alive, as we sit together, here right now, and talk. That's of course, not possible when people are dead. But I now understand that as long as I'm alive, they are alive, too. Of course I cannot have a physical confrontation with them, but the mental relationship is still there.

PROMPTER

Is this how we'll perceive the Unconscious City?

THE ARCHITECT

In previous times people made master plans. I've always said I don't like master plans. I still feel that way. What I do like though, is a strategic device. What is the strategic device, of today? Of tomorrow?

house looked like *that*. They tried to make everything into a typological construct, which I don't believe in. Rather, I believe much more in fluidity; where situations can dissolve, and disappear.

In 1955, when Gerrit Rietveld said that, maybe, walls of a building in the future will consist of magnetic fields–the idea of dematerialized architecture was born. Why should we discuss form when discussing architecture? Why should we talk about blurbs and blobs? That's not the world we live in. Blurbs and blobs do not mirror or mimic nature; they are artificial constructs. Oppositely, and interestingly (and increasingly), buildings do not need to look as if they mimic nature, in order to actually do so. Collective memory must be completely reinterpreted. We have to think about these issues in a very different way, because our collective memory changes every day. When a single product is introduced to the world that progresses communication, globally, our collective memory will change. Events like these alter the ways in which we remember human history. It is more than likely that we will acknowledge a collective unconscious. A few years ago my father passed away, and shortly thereafter my mother passed way. I've learned a lot about death during the past years. I've learned that life is instant. Life is fluid. And yet people always treat life as if *this* or *that* will determine the outcome.

There is a physical aspect to being alive, as we sit together, here right now, and talk. That's of course, not possible when people are dead. But I now understand that as long as I'm alive, they are alive, too. Of course I cannot have a physical confrontation with them, but the mental relationship is still there.

PROMPTER

Is this how we'll perceive the Unconscious City?

THE ARCHITECT

In previous times people made master plans. I've always said I don't like master plans. I still feel that way. What I do like though, is a strategic device. What is the strategic device, of today? Of tomorrow?

PROMPTER

But how do we make a strategic device for a city; for many cities?

THE ARCHITECT

When Barcelona hosted the Olympic Games, and the city said: 'We'll bring the city to the sea.' That, to me, was a strategic device. Only after such a device is conceived can cities begin to become multi-layered conditions. Or like in 1964, in Tokyo. When the Olympic Games were staged, the city discovered it had an infrastructural challenge. What did they do? They brought traffic and highways into Tokyo, and into very radical and very crude spaces, mostly along buildings. But one thing they didn't do was put streets on the 'ground floor' of the city and block the flow. And, since they didn't do that, the city, on the 'ground floor' is still very much connected. It's possible to walk across Tokyo. Subways are multi-layered, with program underground. Everything is elevated in Tokyo. Yet, in the air, there are highways. That was a strategic device.

When you ask me about programmatic conditions, about programs, I say: Yes. We will keep using words like school, library, and house. We will most certainly continue to use these words. But we must also remember to create new and different definitions that can be applied to such terms. Just as our languages have developed over centuries, so too do our cities.

How do we think about different programmatic conditions – like living and working – the house and the office, or the library, or the theater? How can we create new categories and disconnect them from, what I would call, the old fashioned typological discussion, such as: The house is the home, and the place for that family. And you live in neighborhoods, where people are at home. Or, there's a library, and that's the place where people sit under a big dome, and read. And then there's the theater, and that's a place where there's a stage, and the audience looks at it. My office is currently designing a new theater, and it will be completely different from an approved typology. In that sense, the Elbphilharmonie

in Hamburg, by Herzog de Meuron, is probably one of the most beautiful buildings in the world; when I attended the opening the multi-focused acoustic seemed the greatest achievement. And, of course, it has cost quite a few hundred million Euros. However it's still the old typology of the theater. Architects must rethink the ways of theaters. The theater should first and foremost function in a perfect way as a theater, but the structure itself has changed and will change. We must question what exactly a theater is at this moment in time. Are audiences still sitting passively and looking at one stage? Or could we perhaps have multiple stages? Is the seating area moving, rising, or rotating? Beside these questions, we should challenge the fact that the theater as a building serves more program and is an active part of the act during that day. How do we deal with this challenge, as architects?
As I just said, we're working on a new theater. A moving theater in which the stage and people both move. It will create a completely new experience and challenge to those who produce new performances. I've been discussing and thinking with the client as to how we could develop this new theater for about three years. That's my goal for my next few decades: to create an Unconscious City in which we begin to think about strategic devices based on an individual infrastructural strategy. That's what we should do. And then, we should name it. I've believed, since I was a student, in naming. I've believed, since I was a student, in the word. I've believed, since I was a student, in scenarios. I've believed, since I was a student, in the narrative, which is open. A narrative will be my propaganda for the creation of the Unconscious City: that the city will become fluid, not connected to form, and developed alongside strategies.

That's also my goal in my office right now, and of course, it's very difficult. Is the Hedge House, which is a small hybrid-art gallery that I designed in the Netherlands, part of that? Yes. That project's site was dictated by restrictions; we couldn't build an art gallery, but we could build a house for chickens, for orchids, for garden tools and an orangery. It is now part of Maastricht's Bonnefanten Museum. And so we decided, "Why not do just that? Why not let the chickens live in a space where they can be admired while ity

in Hamburg, by Herzog de Meuron, is probably one of the most beautiful buildings in the world; when I attended the opening the multi-focused acoustic seemed the greatest achievement. And, of course, it has cost quite a few hundred million Euros. However, it's still the old typology of the theater. Architects must rethink the ways of theaters. The theater should first and foremost function in a perfect way as a theater, but the structure itself has changed and will change. We must question what exactly a theater is at this moment in time. Are audiences still sitting passively and looking at one stage? Or could we perhaps have multiple stages? Is the seating area moving, rising, or rotating? Beside these questions, we should challenge the fact that the theater as a building serves more program and is an active part of the act during that day. How do we deal with this challenge, as architects? As I just said, we're working on a new theater. A moving theater in which the stage and people both move. It will create a completely new experience and challenge to those who produce new performances. I've been discussing and thinking with the client as to how we could develop this new theater for about three years. That's my goal for my next few decades: to create an Unconscious City in which we begin to think about strategic devices based on an individual infrastructural strategy. That's what we should do. And then, we should name it. I've believed, since I was a student, in naming. I've believed, since I was a student, in the word. I've believed, since I was a student, in scenarios. I've believed, since I was a student, in the narrative, which is open. A narrative will be my propaganda for the creation of the Unconscious City: that the city will become fluid, not connected to form, and developed alongside strategies.

That's also my goal in my office right now, and of course, it's very difficult. Is the Hedge House, which is a small hybrid-art gallery that I designed in the Netherlands, part of that? Yes. That project's site was dictated by restrictions; we couldn't build an art gallery, but we could build a house for chickens, for orchids, for garden tools and an orangery. It is now part of Maastricht's Bonnefanten Museum. And so we decided, 'Why not do just that? Why not let the chickens live in a space where they can be admired while liv-

ing, alongside the art collected by the owners?' Some people laughed off the idea, at first. But that project is only a preliminary example of what I would like to eventually achieve more of in my own work. The Utrecht University Library, which I designed and is also in the Netherlands, is in that sense, a preliminary example of what I think a library could be. The same is true of the Euroborg Stadium, in Groningen, which includes housing, offices, shops, and retail spaces. I don't say that it's perfect, but it is an example of what I believe the Unconscious City should, or could, be. And people don't only go there for football games; they go there for many reasons. Mainly, to live. It's the same with a new museum my office is designing, and two apartment towers in Bahrain. I'm trying to get away from the classic museum, the white box, and the neutral box. That neutrality often needs a kind of specificity. There are a lot of issues to solve in this project, and I like that. We are no longer living in the twentieth century; the buildings we build should acknowledge that. The skin of the apartment towers open and close like a flower when needed, since nine months a year the temperature allows people to live outside three months a year, when it is not above 50 C.

PROMPTER

I have some questions on the subjects you've just spoken of. They're actually more so comments than questions. The first one is about the physical aspect of your relationship to your parents. I completely understood when you described a memory that doesn't depend on physicality. One could take this to also mean that the physical is not important. And I would like to state that this relationship is very heavily dependent on the long history of the physical connection. So it's not that easy to just say: the physical is not relevant.

THE ARCHITECT

I didn't say that we should take down the Pantheon. I said the Pantheon is great–it's fantastic. But when I'm in a city, like Rome,

looking at the Pantheon, I try, at that very moment, to look at it precisely and intuitively.

'Preferences and feelings as unconscious guides to the present evolution (as well as early learning and culture) influences our preferences and, through them, our tendencies to approach or avoid aspects of our environment. We are predisposed to prefer certain objects and aspects of our own environment over others. We are often guided by our feelings, intuitions, and gut reactions, which prioritize the things that are important to do or attend to.'

—John A. Bargh and Ezequiel Morsella, "The Unconscious Mind," *Perspectives on Psychological Science* 3, no. 1 (2008): 73–79.

THE ARCHITECT

I didn't say that I don't like the Pantheon, but I don't think that the monument, as a physical thing, is that important. Rather, it's a witness to the past. But most of us see monuments as very serious. But one should not make them too important. It lames one. When people start to say: 'Look at how good *this* is when we do something now.' When that happens there is a real danger. That's also the risk. Toward the end of their lives, people often become more and more historical, referencing their own history.

looking at the Pantheon, I try, at that very moment, to look at it precisely and intuitively.

‘Preferences and feelings as unconscious guides to the present evolution (as well as early learning and culture) influences our preferences and, through them, our tendencies to approach or avoid aspects of our environment. We are predisposed to prefer certain objects and aspects of our own environment over others. We are often guided by our feelings, intuitions, and gut reactions, which prioritize the things that are important to do or attend to.’

—John A. Bargh and Ezequiel Morsella, ‘The Unconscious Mind’, *Perspectives on Psychological Science* 3, no. 1 (2008): 73-79.

THE ARCHITECT

I didn’t say that I don’t like the Pantheon, but I don’t think that the monument, as a physical thing, is that important. Rather, it’s a witness to the past. But most of us see monuments as very serious. But one should not make them too important. It lames one. When people start to say: ‘Look at how good *this* is when we do something now.’ When that happens, there is a real danger. That’s also the risk. Toward the end of their lives, people often become more and more historical, referencing their own history.

05:15:00

That's the risk of many architects. Many of them did fantastic experiments in their early years. The Pantheon is great, but it's not something I see as being important to my own work.

I am intrigued by the fact that the Pantheon's program has changed many times. Built as a temple, however, the structure was very different from other traditional temples. Fascinating is the engineering part of it; how the Romans used lighter materials at its top, staring with travertine, brick, and finally pumice. That the oculus allows the sun to flow through the circle, and how the rain runs out of the convex floor, is daring and impressive. It's true that, today, I'm not able to speak to my father and get an actual response from him, in the physical sense of the word. But I believe I can talk to my father in the present. I'm not only referring to the past. I understand now that I can share, and I can talk about, for instance, my sketch for a theater. I can explain it to my father, in the present. I believe thinking is talking out loud, in your own interiority. Designing for me is thinking in words. And thinking is speaking. But you don't speak out loud; you speak to yourself. If I were talking to you, and I had a pen and a piece of paper, I could sketch a theater the way I want it to be. And I can talk to you about it in words. Just last Friday, I talked to people in my office about a theater, and I now know how we are going to do it. It took me longer than a year. That doesn't mean that the design is finished, but the strategy for the design is there. I know what the two or three key elements of the new theater will be. But that doesn't mean I already know how its exterior will look, or which materials will be used. And I don't yet know how tall or wide it will be, but strategically I know how it works. Although we can build it with the help of craftsmen; they add another layer to our strategy, to our idea of how to build, and how to make it. You had more questions...

PROMPTER

The craftsmen. Interesting... Concerning this theater, you speak about an approved typology of the theater, and about reinventing the way in which we perceive and think about theaters.

Why is this the architect's task? Isn't it the task of the stage directors to rethink the notion of a theater? Wouldn't a new building typology, for a theater, come after there's a new way of making a theater? If the stage director's theater is the way they are used to working, I would not, spontaneously, see a need to redo it.

THE ARCHITECT

That's a good question. But it's the same as saying: It's the client, the inhabitant of the house who should know how the house would best be used. Some architects, of course, think this way. It's the inhabitant of the theater, or the library, for instance, who should know these things. But I can tell you, they don't. But they can help. Mrs. Farnsworth was extremely important to Mies van der Rohe while making the Farnsworth House. If Mies hadn't had so many lunches with her, he would never have made it that way. Though, that doesn't mean she told him what to do. I've been speaking with my clients for two years about making this particular theater. We talk and we talk, and we stop and then we meet, and talk again. But without meeting, without a client, I can't even begin to think about a new project. I created a dialogue; the better the questions are, the more I am challenged. As an architect, I can't do everything alone. That's why I utilize a dialogue. By being asked questions, I have to rephrase, rethink. And when a client and I see one another in person, an atmosphere is created. This is essential for true dialogue. If I wouldn't have this relationship with my client for this theater, or for a museum, the theater and the museum would never be built. We both have to challenge one another. That's why I, more and more, disbelieve in competitions, because they contain no dialogue with clients. A competition can most often only be used as an intermediate step. I see that in my office. When we do a competition for a library, I do not know the client. I can do something, but I always feel a little bit frustrated, because I'll always try to find the client. Competitions do not offer this dialogue. I need to know who my client is, and what they think.

Why is this the architect's task? Isn't it the task of the stage directors to rethink the notion of a theater? Wouldn't a new building typology, for a theater, come after there's a new way of making a theater? If the stage director's theater is the way they are used to working, I would not, spontaneously, see a need to redo it.

THE ARCHITECT

That's a good question. But it's the same as saying: It's the client, the inhabitant of the house who should know how the house would best be used. Some architects, of course, think this way. It's the inhabitant of the theater, or the library, for instance, who should know these things. But I can tell you, they don't. But they can help. Mrs. Farnsworth was extremely important to Mies van der Rohe while making the Farnsworth House. If Mies hadn't had so many lunches with her, he would never have made it that way. Though, that doesn't mean she told him what to do. I've been speaking with my clients for two years about making this particular theater. We talk and we talk, and we stop and then we meet, and talk again. But without meeting, without a client, I can't even begin to think about a new project. I created a dialogue; the better the questions are, the more I am challenged. As an architect, I can't do everything alone. That's why I utilize a dialogue. By being asked questions, I have to rephrase, rethink. And when a client and I see one another in person, an atmosphere is created. This is essential for true dialogue. If I wouldn't have this relationship with my client for this theater, or for a museum, the theater and the museum would never be built. We both have to challenge one another. That's why I, more and more, disbelieve in competitions, because they contain no dialogue with clients. A competition can most often only be used as an intermediate step. I see that in my office. When we do a competition for a library, I do not know the client. I can do something, but I always feel a little bit frustrated, because I'll always try to find the client. Competitions do not offer this dialogue. I need to know who my client is, and what they think.

Even if we were to only talk about soccer, that's important to me. I need that dialogue. And that's why *Politeia* is so important to me, too. As are the three books of *Eupalinos: or, The Architect*. After having this format of a dialogue, I usually think that the client and I will do something great together, because I can't create or make something, out of the nothing. I recently designed a cutlery set with Alessi; it was launched in 2014. The dialogue with Alberto Alessi began with a sketch of mine, and after meeting I changed it a bit according to his reaction, by doing more sketches. This process will be repeated several times until we arrive at a design influenced and developed by both of us, which we both believed in. I can't make the cutlery by sitting for three weeks in an attic and working on it. We are living in a time with a constantly changing, fluid, and collective memory. What is this collective memory the moment I do a theater or a museum? In 2014, during the building process of the Allianz Headquarters in Zürich, I constantly changed aspects of the design according to my dialogues with the client. I have to talk to the client again, and again, and I'm still not sure about some changes. But I need this confrontation with the client to have a debate about the way they will use the building, and organize their company. I initiate a dialogue about the *Arbeitswelten*, partly based on my readings of Ernst Jünger, who believed in the value of the individual.

PROMPTER

You previously referred to Tokyo, and how its highways were built so that they wouldn't interrupt the fabric of the city. What's a ground floor condition? Is it the program of a city?

THE ARCHITECT

That's a very good, and difficult, question. I held a lecture series a few years ago with titles like: 'Zero Zero Level', 'Multiple Zero Level', and 'Multiple Levels', or the skin of the Earth with burning lava is what fascinates me; eruptions and a sense of danger. All of these refer to my idea of the ground floor. The ground floor is, for every human being, this kind of moment: 'OK, here I have vast ground.' I can't explain it any differently. It's being on Earth –

quite literally being on the ground. Strange enough, we just opened a building. People were sitting in the café, and they all thought they were on ground floor, but they weren't. A 'zero level' is connected to the ground; that's number one. Number two is that it's fake. Most of the Netherlands' 'ground' is actually water. So the 'ground floor' is the place where you feel stable, and, in a city, also where there is the impression that this ground floor has never actually ended. I think it was very clever of Tokyo to create a kind of instant continuity of the city's fabric under its elevated highways. When people accept a particular level as ground floor, they feel safe, without having the problem of going above or below it. The moment a second 'zero level' is created, there will still be a feeling of being elevated or below ground. The continuity is gone, and people don't like that. Continuity is important, even if it's artificial. It probably has more to do with human perception. If a stable condition in a city is created, let's call it the 'ground floor', that would be an incredibly important strategic device for that city. But you can also decide to bring people into an unstable and strange condition, and it can help. It can challenge them. It simply has to do with the idea: I take people away from it. If I'm driving in Tokyo, I'm simply on an autonomous structure. I don't drive there, as I would in Omotesando, or Ginza, where people can pass by and I can look into shops. By elevating its highways, Tokyo created an independent level, within its urbanity. I imagine that what I'm trying to say is that it's very important to bring a city's population into either a stable and/or unstable environment, depending on the momentum.

PROMPTER

If we consider people using highways in Tokyo as exposed to a potentially unstable but fast changing condition, how does this condition then relate to speed within a city?

THE ARCHITECT

This is perhaps a completely different example, but in the Jelly-fish House, a house we completed in Los Monteros, Spain, we

quite literally being on the ground. Strange enough, we just opened a building. People were sitting in the café, and they all thought they were on ground floor, but they weren't. A 'zero level' is connected to the ground; that's number one. Number two is that it's fake. Most of the Netherlands' 'ground' is actually water. So the 'ground floor' is the place where you feel stable, and in a city, also where there is the impression that this ground floor has never actually ended. I think it was very clever of Tokyo, to create a kind of instant continuity of the city's fabric under its elevated highways. When people accept a particular level as ground floor, they feel safe, without having the problem of going above or below it. The moment a second 'zero level' is created, there will still be a feeling of being elevated or below ground. The continuity is gone, and people don't like that. Continuity is important, even if it's artificial. It probably has more to do with human perception. If a stable condition in a city is created, let's call it the 'ground floor'; that would be an incredibly important strategic device for that city. But you can also decide to bring people into an unstable and strange condition, and it can help. It can challenge them. It simply has to do with the idea: I take people away from it. If I'm driving in Tokyo, I'm simply on an autonomous structure. I don't drive there, as I would in Omotesandō, or Ginza, where people can pass by and I can look into shops. By elevating its highways, Tokyo created an independent level, within its urbanity. I imagine that what I'm trying to say is that it's very important to bring a city's population into either a stable and/or unstable environment, depending on the momentum.

PROMPTER

If we consider people using highways in Tokyo as exposed to a potentially unstable but fast changing condition, how does this condition then relate to speed within a city?

THE ARCHITECT

This is perhaps a completely different example, but in the Jellyfish House, a house we completed in Los Monteros, Spain, we,

we created stairs with different slopes. There are differences in how one approaches, or how one communicates, on very steep stairs. Everything is different on each stair. I'm interested in the idea that we should be more aware of speed. Fast, and slow... The routing in the Utrecht University Library is also based on speed and the moment of rest, of standing still. Words like speed, and the development of the ground floor, are strategic devices within a city. For instance, if I'm in Tokyo, I walk from one patch of fabric to the next, and if there's a highway in between, it's there. I don't care. And of course there are also streets on the ground floor in Tokyo, busy streets. But somehow it feels different; it's not such a cut. In a city like Tokyo, the underground – regardless of how many levels one is below ground – is developed as a condition of being inside. In almost any department store in Tokyo there is an absolute unawareness of the floor level. And I only perceive this condition in Tokyo in many different circumstances. I'm somewhere in an interior, but where exactly, I never quite know. I have no idea on which floor I am, where north is... And that's the reason why underground systems in Tokyo work so well. They give the feeling that they're so vast that one could walk endlessly in any direction. It's not like being in a tunnel. And it only works when it's strategic. I'm not sure if they ever thought about this in Tokyo. Maybe they did a few trial and error tests. But there is no other city in the world where the underground world, with millions of square meters of shopping and theaters and spaces, functions as it does in Tokyo. Though of any other city, perhaps Montréal has a glimpse of it. This 'zero-level' also involves the idea of scale – the very big skyscraper next to the little house. Or speed. In the Unconscious City, these defining moments are there, and they can be played with, but one is not always aware, that there are different speeds in the house, or that it is possible to be in a completely internal condition – the complete ground floor condition. We must be aware of these conditions. Human beings have changed over the last decades a lot. We are able to perceive our very complex world in such a way that we can cope with it. Our city will become more complex. Our houses and buildings will become more complex, because we can cope with this change. If someone from

the nineteenth century today walked through the city center of Tokyo, they would, quite literally, go crazy within two hours. But the new city is connected to new technology. Soon the city will be a driverless city as transportation systems automate and serve individuals in a collective society. The complexity of this new technology is related to the complexity of our new world. There is an unconscious condition connected to the complexity of technology, and I believe the same is true of our cities.

PROMPTER

Would you state that the world needs rules to achieve these unconscious conditions in other cities?

THE ARCHITECT

We are almost always in an unconscious condition. How can we as designers and architects work with that unconsciousness? I strongly believe that people are no longer interested in the discussion of facades. That's passé. Does a building work, does it function, and does it provide its inhabitants with something, is it challenging? One of the biggest questions for architects is: How can we make a building that lasts longer than three years? That's why I say we should develop buildings that have a second and a third life. In cities we should not say: 'You are allowed to do this here, you are not allowed to do this there.' I'm not for total urban design freedom, but rather for freedom within strategic rules. And these rules will be created within the next years. Our cities will become cities in which we formulate a few strict rules, and forget all others. The idea that there is one person in the urban department of a city, who can dictate what its citizens can and can't do, is no longer of our time. Big ideas sometimes worked out very well in the past, with trusted architects, urban planners, artists, engineers, and philosophers. I still believe in such hierarchies. New cities will be democratic cities, but democratic in the old definition of the word: there is freedom and there are rules, a few rules, which can be interpreted in many ways, like the Bible, or the Koran. I still believe that what will dramatically change in the next few years is the idea of the manual. For that, Steve Jobs has been incredible; because he

05:28:30

the nineteenth century today walked through the city center of Tokyo, they would, quite literally, go crazy within two hours. But the new city is connected to new technology. Soon the city will be a driverless city as transportation systems automate and serve individuals in a collective society. The complexity of this new technology is related to the complexity of our new world. There is an unconscious condition connected to the complexity of technology, and I believe the same is true of our cities.

PROMPTER

Would you state that the world needs rules to achieve these unconscious conditions in other cities?

THE ARCHITECT

We are almost always in an unconscious condition. How can we as designers and architects work with that unconsciousness? I strongly believe that people are no longer interested in the discussion of façades. That's passé. Does a building work, does it function, and does it provide its inhabitants with something, is it challenging? One of the biggest questions for architects is: How can we make a building that lasts longer than three years? That's why I say we should develop buildings that have a second and a third life. In cities we should not say: 'You are allowed to do this here, you are not allowed to do this there.' I'm not for total urban design freedom, but rather for freedom within strategic rules. And these rules will be created within the next years. Our cities will become cities in which we formulate a few strict rules, and forget all others. The idea that there is one person in the urban department of a city, who can dictate what its citizens can and can't do, is no longer of our time. Big ideas sometimes worked out very well in the past, with trusted architects, urban planners, artists, engineers, and philosophers. I still believe in such hierarchies. New cities will be democratic cities, but democratic in the old definition of the word: there is freedom and there are rules, a few rules, which can be interpreted in many ways, like the Bible, or the Koran. I still believe that what will dramatically change in the next few years is the idea of the manual. For that, Steve Jobs has been incredible; because he

developed Apple and the iPhone; they used the icon, which is so simple. It just works. For all the other tools and technology, up until a few years ago, manuals were needed to understand how a product worked. That's because they were poorly designed. And that's still the case with the way cities have been developed over the last half decade, and it's something in which I no longer believe. I still believe in rules, like the one in Berlin, that previously stated that buildings cannot be higher than 23 m, although even though it limited the big idea that Berlin was about to be. That's what I like about Tokyo, that there are only two rules: the zoning law and earthquake law. For the rest, architects can do whatever they want. That's what our collective memory now wants us to do. Our collective memory is no longer only asking for façades.

One more point on this topic; I believe in youth, in young people. The old society was the society of the grey, the wise. I still accept that, in a certain way. But the dynamic of the young was not able, twenty or thirty years ago. So when speaking about the new city, I'm also speaking about the city of the young: the blonde city. I'm not saying that the grey city is not there. It certainly is, in Barcelona, Paris or Rome, for instance. But Tokyo is a 'blonde city', a city of the young, the dynamic, the uncontrolled, the undefined, and the unconscious. Respect is still a big word to be conscious of, when dealing with the city today. It is probably the closest way of getting to a collective attitude of refreshing our rules, and of getting to 'an architecture of freedom'. When walking with Kazuo Shinohara, during my first trip to Japan in 1983, we had lunch close to the Shibuya station and he explained to me his idea of chaos, anarchism, myth, and the beauty of the ugliness of the city of Tokyo.

'I am an ephemeral and not too discontent citizen of a raw modern city.'
—Rimbaud, *Les Illumination*

05:30:45

'The form of a city, Baudelaire noted with irony and some nostalgia in the face of Haussmann's reconstructive fury, changes more quickly than the heart of a mortal. But, as successive "modernisms" and "counter-modernisms" have demonstrated, often the heart changes even more quickly than the city itself. Le Corbusier's impatience at the obstinate survival of old Paris—"Imagine this junk, which till now has lain spread out over the soil like a dry crust, cleaned off and carted away"—is only one extreme example of the radical shifts in the sensibility toward the city in this century, shifts that have more often than not been resisted by the intractable nature of the existing urban fabric.'

—Anthony Vidler, *The Architectural Uncanny: Essays in the Modern Unhomely* (Cambridge: MIT Press, 1992), 199.

05:33:00

‘The form of a city, Baudelaire noted with irony and some nostalgia in the face of Haussmann’s reconstructive fury, changes more quickly than the heart of a mortal. But, as successive “modernisms” and “counter-modernisms” have demonstrated, often the heart changes even more quickly than the city itself. Le Corbusier’s impatience at the obstinate survival of old Paris—“Imagine this junk, which till now has lain spread out over the soil like a dry crust, cleaned off and carted away”—is only one extreme example of the radical shifts in the sensibility toward the city in this century, shifts that have more often than not been resisted by the intractable nature of the existing urban fabric.’

—Anthony Vidler, *The Architectural Uncanny: Essays in Modern Unhomely* (Cambridge: MIT Press, 1992), 199.

05:33:00

PROMPTER

If I refer once more to the collective memory, which could also be seen as a collective present or collective future, by isolating the term 'collective', I wonder what it would look like? If we don't need anyone to determine how a city should look, where is the collective?

THE ARCHITECT

Everyone should make a difference. In the old days, the collective was the community of the village, the church, etc., but also as manifested by painters, philosophers, and writers. They had – and in some tribes of the world one can still see this – rituals. The collective always has to do with rituals; it has to do with songs and stories and storytelling. Collective memory means that it is built up and transferred from one generation to the next. But our time has changed dramatically, and perhaps there still is a collective, but with another collective next to it, and another next to that. Times have changed; it is now possible to be a part of many different groups, and suddenly we could lose responsibility, the criticism, since it is now more and more a time of the 'self', the 'I', and one is now able to hope to escape. I called it the club-city, but maybe it's also the collective city. You are Christian or Muslim or Jewish or atheist, but no matter which religion-club you identify with, you can still enjoy hockey, and also be in the hockey-club, and the architect-club, and still be a fan of Manchester United, for instance. In the old understanding of clubs, all people lived in the same area, they were all fans of Liverpool, or all Catholic, or all dressed in a certain way. That's the collective memory, the way we talked about it, let's say, until the year 2000. But from 2000 onward, the collective has dispersed. The world has become a collective city and since part of a wider universe, I would like to called our world the 'cosmopolis'; with neighborhoods we call 'megapoli' or 'metropoli'. We are able to travel to the Moon and beyond; the cosmos are stretching with each new discovery in the solar system. The history of Rome, the memory of the Roman, was connected to the Roman Empire, which for them, was the history of the world. It would be great,

if I, as an architect, would be able to understand where the common sense is in this diversity. Maybe it's in the iPhone, because it's so neutral on the one hand, and so specific on the other. It becomes acceptable for everyone. And it's not even connected to a social status, because at a certain moment, everyone will have one. Though at first, it was very much connected to social status, when it was first introduced in 2007. And 2007 was a monumental year, in retrospect; we forget that all too easily, but it's the year the iPhone was launched, and the year that proved to be the tipping point, of what eventually became the 'Great Recession'. Then, the iPhone became neutral; a platform, an interactive platform by which everything is interconnected. That's also interesting for buildings.

PROMPTER

I could imagine going one step further, because the word 'club' still makes it sound as if somebody is very aware of being a member of it. I would instead call it common. You have an iPhone, he has an iPhone, and you are not a club, but you both have something in common. I'm Christian, he is Christian, but we never celebrate our Christianity together. A lot of interests overlap; it's more like attributes, as opposed to circles.

THE ARCHITECT

The internet is a network of networks. Since 1969, ARPANET carried its first packet, and it was possible for a select few to communicate indifferent from where they were; independent from place and time.

PROMPTER

If you join a group on Facebook, such as the 'It's-hard-to-get-up-in-the-morning' group, you don't want to share your experience with others and talk about your unpleasant morning routines. You just use it as an attribute to define

your personality. That's why I think it's less being part of a club, and instead an exercise in collecting attributes. We are entering an era of identity driven societies; political, and apolitical.

THE ARCHITECT

That's correct, and it's the same with a hockey-club. You play hockey because your sister plays it, or for any other reason. But the big difference in the ways in which we now talk about a club, and fifty years ago, is that it was then obligatory. You had to be Catholic if you lived in Munich, for instance. But now, everything is left to free will, and it's your choice. I see it with my son; he's constantly doing different things, he is this with one friend, and he is that with another. He is fan of Ajax, Amsterdam's football team, but also a fan of his local team. It was not like this fifty years ago. If your parents were bakers, you became, most likely, a baker. If your parents were part of this political party, you most likely also became part of it, too. And when you didn't, you were an outcast. But when my son would do the same as I have, I would think: 'Is there something wrong with you?' We are living in a time of free will; make your own choices! Of course friends, family, and media and so on influence us all. But at least, we can choose. That's why I once wrote, in one of my texts, club-city, but also choice-city. I believe very strongly in choice-city. We, as architects, should make a book about choices. But again, here is the idea of choice, and I think you have to be specific. At school, 'sport' is no longer a class, since it creates tension; some students are good at it, and other less so. For me, that students no longer take sporting classes as part of their primary education is impossible to fathom, since the act of training our bodies is one of the most important and challenging acts of all. Here, individualism is at the edge. You should not fail. Yet today everyone gets a gold medal, so there is no competition. Even in classrooms no one can fail. It may mark the end of education and universities, since you will get your diploma after you pay. A free ticket makes the ride useless. The time when you bought Legos for your kids is no more. Lego is bankrupt, or will perhaps one day be. Why? Even you, as kids, probably had Legos. And suddenly

they're gone. Young children are not interested in Legos anymore. They are not hands-on enough. They are, but in a very different way. That's a big difference within today's society. I don't say that time is forever gone, but at this moment, I don't see it. Most very interesting people, like Steve Jobs, skip school altogether and educate themselves. That is, by the way, what Tadao Ando messaged when, at the start of the Berlage institute, he refused to give a master class, because he had been a kick boxer, and understood that training, competition, have always worked and that self-education is what success is all about. When the Unconscious City develops, we must be aware of the fact that our society has changed. People have different interests, and so they all need different products. When we talk about program, it has to do with products. You can't develop a product for which you haven't defined the program. So, we have to develop them.

PROMPTER

Does this influence the way we live and the way we use certain programs within our homes?

THE ARCHITECT

Begin by asking questions:

Do you sit with them and talk? Is this new apartment a place where you would take friends? Or is it a place that looks like a recording studio? Or is there a large screen on your wall, like at the NYSE, to communicate through new medias with your friends? What is the program of the new house? You can sleep there, but what is your bedroom about? Or take, for instance, the kitchen. What are you cooking? And how often? The kitchen was designed for daily routines, but that's gone. Ninety per cent of people no longer live in traditional nuclear families. So when the routine of daily cooking has disappeared, in the way that we previously knew it, we can think about kitchens differently. We designed a kitchen with Alessi, which is lanched in 2014 – a different, new kitchen. It doesn't look quite like a kitchen at all; maybe there is also a bed in the new kitchen. And the bathroom is maybe in the living room. I even think that these words will disappear: bathroom, living room, and

they're gone. Young children are not interested in Legos anymore. They are not hands-on enough. They are, but in a very different way. That's a big difference within today's society. I don't say that time is forever gone, but at this moment, I don't see it. Most very interesting people, like Steve Jobs, skip school altogether and educate themselves. That is, by the way, what Tadao Ando messaged when, at the start of the Berlage Institute, he refused to give a master class, because he had been a kick-boxer, and understood that training, competition, have always worked and that self education is what success is all about. When the Unconscious City develops, we must be aware of the fact that our society has changed. People have different interests, and so they all need different products. When we talk about program, it has to do with products. You can't develop a product, for which you haven't defined the program. So, we have to develop them.

PROMPTER

Does this influence the way we live and the way we use certain programs within our homes?

THE ARCHITECT

Begin by asking questions:

Do you sit with them and talk? Is this new apartment a place where you would take friends? Or is it a place that looks like a recording studio? Or is there a large screen on your wall, like at the NYSE, to communicate through new medias with your friends? What is the program of the new house? You can sleep there, but what is your bedroom about? Or take, for instance, the kitchen. What are you cooking? And how often? The kitchen was designed for daily routines, but that's gone. Ninety per cent of people no longer live in traditional nuclear families. So when the routine of daily cooking has disappeared, in the way that we previously knew it, we can think about kitchens differently. We designed a kitchen with Alessi, which launched in 2014 – a different, new kitchen. It doesn't look quite like a kitchen at all; maybe there is also a bed in the new kitchen. And the bathroom is maybe in the living room. I even think that these words will disappear: bathroom, living room, and

kitchen. I can raise a lot of questions that I can't answer, yet. But I strongly believe that it's in our interest to think about these issues, because our relationship to food, to buying, preparing, and cooking, have all changed. A lot of people eat as I do; they eat more than half of their meals in restaurants. But if I cook at home, I enjoy it. I invite my friends over for dinner and give them a 'silver spoon' as a present. Everybody could bring something; we eat and talk about the food we're cooking. It's great. It is a collective experience that we can share with friends, facilitated by our contemporary media, even as it's possible to have it disconnected from our focus.

PROMPTER

In our earlier discussion on 'Infra' – chapter four – you mentioned that home could be anywhere. Does this also relate to urban programs, and require a change? Or, at least require us to not stop questioning them?

THE ARCHITECT

It's also the sharing-city. Of course, we shared before, but then it was hierarchical. So, to share things, to choose, to club; these actions are part of how I believe we should discuss the now city – the Unconscious City – and products, to work or live with, and within. We should openly discuss challenges and opportunities. There was a big problem in the Netherlands in the late 1990s, when I was the Dean of the Berlage Institute. One million houses were to be built in the Netherlands, and many recently graduated young architects built their first projects. But no one challenged the typology of the house: the house with a garden where two people with two children and a dog live. It was only camouflage; one made a red house, one a blue house, one with a flat roof, one in stones, etc... There was absolutely no debate about the house. People built villages with 20,000 or 30,000 homes, or more, which are sleepy, disconnected areas of the Netherlands – without infrastructure, and collective facilities. Society shouldn't do that. It was a major opportunity, with a tragic outcome. We have been strongly against this idea of Vinex, and even initiated at the Berlage Institute the study theme of 'Double Dutch' to

challenge the possibilities of such growth. Every time we receive a commission in my office, we restart a debate about the potential of the commission. It was the same in Studio Arets at the UdK. Whatever students did, it was up to them. It was their responsibility. I'm not a professor that will tell students what to do. I can tell them what I think about their work. But however young they are, the moment they enter the university, they are architects. They begin school as architecture students; yet they are already architects. In the last studio at the UdK we worked on a Manhattan project: they challenged one another to raise questions, and to slowly develop a concept, a strategy, for interfering with Manhattan. It's strange that our discipline is rather slow and architects don't like taking risks. Not risks in terms of form or shape, but risks in terms of trying to do something fundamentally different. The Boeing airplane hasn't fundamentally changed over the last fifty years. It's still flying with the same speed. But that will change when we cross the border of 1,000 km/h. We will soon fly via orbit from Amsterdam to Tokyo in three hours. Also, by the Zeppelin, using the same route, but in thirty hours. High speed versus slowness. The Concorde was a first-try-out, but the only difference was the speed. The introduction of the iPhone in 2007 crossed a border in communication. For a long time Nokia was the leader in mobile phones. They introduced new colors, new shapes, a few little changes here and there, every now and then. But then phones suddenly changed, fundamentally, with the iPhone. I think this could also happen in architecture. And soon. At least we should challenge ourselves to enable this to occur.

PROMPTER

If this fundamental shift were to happen in architecture, would it spur from a generic device?

THE ARCHITECT

It's both generic and specific. We should be very careful about the word generic. It most often has a tricky connotation. In the pharmaceutical industry, it means a copied product, and not the original.

05:46:30

challenge the possibilities of such growth. Every time we receive a commission in my office, we restart a debate about the potential of the commission. It was the same in Studio Arets at the UdK. Whatever students did, it was up to them. It was their responsibility. I'm not a professor that will tell students what to do. I can tell them what I think about their work. But however young they are, the moment they enter the university, they are architects. They begin school as architecture students; yet they are already architects. In the last studio at the UdK we worked on a Manhattan project; they challenged one another to raise questions, and to slowly develop a concept, a strategy, for interfering with Manhattan.
It's strange that our discipline is rather slow and architects don't like taking risks. Not risks in terms of form or shape, but risks in terms of trying to do something fundamentally different. The Boeing airplane hasn't fundamentally changed over the last fifty years. It's still flying with the same speed. But that will change when we cross the border of 1,000 km/h. We will soon fly via orbit from Amsterdam to Tokyo in three hours. Also, by the Zeppelin, using the same route, but in thirty hours. High speed versus slowness. The Concorde was a first-try-out, but the only difference was the speed. The introduction of the iPhone in 2007 crossed a border in communication. For a long time Nokia was the leader in mobile phones. They introduced new colors, new shapes; a few little changes here and there, every now and then. But then phones suddenly changed, fundamentally, with the iPhone. I think this could also happen in architecture. And soon. At least we should challenge ourselves to enable this to occur.

PROMPTER

If this fundamental shift were to happen in architecture, would it spur from a generic device?

THE ARCHITECT

It's both generic and specific. We should be very careful about the word generic. It most often has a tricky connotation. In the pharmaceutical industry, it means a copied product, and not the original.

PROMPTER

That's true. But architecture could also be generic in the sense of an old building typology that defines the common way of building. Could you imagine that architecture is a product, like the 'Apple' house?

THE ARCHITECT

Of course. But I don't believe in the new, for the sake of the new. I believe in the new because our collective memory has changed. I'm not against a worldwide collective memory, and we have to understand what the collective is now, in order to fully understand it. We live in a different collective, and it's changing everyday. I never believed in 'the architect'. I believe in Malaparte as an archetype for the architect. He was however, a writer. I don't believe that someone is an architect because he has a diploma. Yet when I go to a heart surgeon, I'd like to know whether they studied and what their curriculum was. I believe in Comme des Garçons. And Porsche. It's tricky with brands, if you extend the brand to a new product, for example. A brand, for me, is a business card. And that business card represents so much more than what's been printed on it. Whatever brands you wear or whatever car you drive, doesn't really matter anyway. It's not really about having the most. Fair is also a good word. The fair-city. The share-city. Yet most of the world today is still organized around a post-code society; addresses still matter.

PROMPTER

Do you think that the share-city or choice-city is a fairer city, with more common values than our cities have now? Will these cities occur automatically?

THE ARCHITECT

I think our world is becoming fairer and fairer. Even in favelas, for example, you can buy a MacBook Pro and be connected to the world. People from favelas are able to study by computer. In the old days, when you were born rich, you were rich. But when

you were born into a poor family, for instance, in the Amazonas, you were poor in the Amazonas. That's changed. The world is becoming fairer, and more fluid. But also less rough. People now have options, and opportunities. But also less competition. We are connected to every spot on the globe and our news is instantaneous in its broadcast. So in fact, everything seems smooth, nice, beautiful, and polished. The world currently lacks resistance and is becoming, in fact, quite bleak.

PROMPTER

It's also more exhausting, and more tempting.
And maybe, a little bit more fun.

THE ARCHITECT

Yes, in comparison to what; what is our reference? And only as long as we create a society of fairness, a society of freedom, and a society that also has rules. But these rules must be collective. That's what's happening in Europe, and all over the world, at the moment. We should have a political agenda, with just a few rules. That's where we should go: a few good rules instead of a whole package of manuals. It is also very important from which viewpoint one is anticipating. Since the West already probably has multiple directions; as well as in the East so there is not only one 'we'! I'm extremely positive about the time we are living in, even though the next decades have the potential to become much more crude, in some respects. More and more people will become educated, and connected, and the debates of the world will become more transparent. Though society will become increasingly more aggressive, as competition between the growing population, increases. It depends on what you are connected to, and to which club is judging your opinion. That was different a century ago. But, maybe it won't matter. When going to a hospital these days, everything is a bit more transparent. When you are ill, you are ill. I don't think that we will live in a society where everyone is equal. Actually, I think differences will grow between social classes, but in a fair way. Everyone has chances. And I hope that those chances will continue to increase. I see the city in the same way: as a place where people have chances. A chance to build

a house, or a production plant. But with only a few rules, like no CO^2, no noise, and no pollution. That's it. And that would be much more exciting. The city, the metropolis, the cosmopolis; the world will change because of great ideas like it always has. Technological innovation will challenge our environment, which will slowly take different appearances. The world of tomorrow starts today, so we must rethink our metropolises. I'm not right wing but I'm also not left wing. Political parties are old fashioned. We have to talk to each other in terms of fairness and respect. It's clear that we don't want excessive noise, or smoke pollution. That's clear, and there should simply be a rule that deals with that. But what are the real philosoph-ical issues we have to look at, instead of minor political dust? What are the real challenges we are confronted with today? Once we deal with innovation in a fair manner and with respect, city life and society in general, will become much more exciting. Our cities will be much more inviting. But they will also create differences, because competition will grow. We are living in a multicultural society, with some parts of the world further integrated than others, in this respect. I'm very happy about this.

I like Japan, even though there is no multiculturalism there, at all. Only three percent of the people in Japan are of non-Japanese decent – they come from abroad. Yet they will never be seen as Japanese by the Japanese, no matter how long they live there or how far they integrate. Yet I also like New York City, where there are hardly any 'Americans' on the street at all. In Manhattan, everyone is from somewhere else. Tokyo is not better than New York City, or the other way around. They're just different, and that's fine. We should encourage respect and innocence. Let us simply be open to change, and changes within our society. We should get rid of the society of fear, a society where many things are not possible. Everything should be possible within set rules. Let us have no fear, for what must we fear? Maybe we should fear for 'decadence', but that topic is not yet on the agenda, even though it could have a substantial impact on the decades to come.

05:55:30

06:00:00

クリクホ㈱
CAT
320E
No.20

HITACHI

司
青

06:00:00 —
07:12:00

UN-C-C

CITIES MUST
PREPARE FOR THE
RADICAL CHANGES
TO COME.

06:02:15

06:00:00 –
07:12:00

UN-C-C

CITIES MUST
PREPARE FOR THE
RADICAL CHANGES
TO COME.

06:02:15

PROMPTER

If we were to state that *L'Architettura della Città* was about the past, while *Vers une Architecture* was about the future, and *Delirious New York* the present; what interests you most: the past, present, or the future?

THE ARCHITECT

Actually, all three books are about the future. The English title of *Vers une Architecture* is *Toward a New Architecture*. It has progressiveness to it, I feel. Le Corbusier's city was Paris, although he was more indifferent about it. Rossi's city seems to be Rome; he talks about the past and present in his volume; he is actually interested in a new city to come, a compact city where the monument occupies a very strong position. And when Koolhaas analyzed New York City, he stated that phenomena like Coney Island, or certain buildings in the city, play a role that's relevant beyond the city's borders. He makes a statement for the future by saying which cities have a chance to survive, and which don't. He is polemic. All three felt as if the city they were preoccupied with could be improved upon.

PROMPTER

Which comes closest to your idea of the future city?

THE ARCHITECT

For me, the future city is Tokyo. It's a city I confront myself with regularly. It's very hard to describe, as well as draw. It's a city without figure: it's a city that one could easily call 'low resolution,' and it's very low-rise, like a carpet. But it has just as much happening underground (like transport and even entire buildings) as it does aboveground. When I speak about unconsciousness, as a city, Tokyo is a place where one can completely concentrate on the task at hand—whatever that may be; conscious awareness of the city one is in. It has a lot to offer and a 24/7 challenging profile, without trying to be loud. Tokyo is not overwhelming. Maybe it is in Shinjuku, or Shibuya; but in general, I think that Tokyo is a city

PROMPTER

If we were to state that *L'Architettura della Città* was about the past, while *Vers une Architecture* was about the future, and *Delirious New York* the present; what interests you most: the past, present, or the future?

THE ARCHITECT

Actually, all three books are about the future. The English title of *Vers une Architecture* is *Toward a New Architecture*. It has progressiveness to it, I feel. Le Corbusier's city was Paris, although he was more indifferent about it. Rossi's city seems to be Rome; he talks about the past and present in his volume, he is actually interested in a new city to come, a compact city where the monument occupies a very strong position. And when Koolhaas analyzed New York City, he stated that phenomena like Coney Island, or certain buildings in the city, play a role that's relevant beyond the city's borders. He makes a statement for the future by saying which cities have a chance to survive, and which don't. He is polemic. All three felt as if the city they were preoccupied with could be improved upon.

PROMPTER

Which comes closest to your idea of the future city?

THE ARCHITECT

For me, the future city is Tokyo. It's a city I confront myself with regularly. It's very hard to describe, as well as draw. It's a city without figure. It's a city that one could easily call 'low resolution', and it's very low-rise, like a carpet. But it has just as much happening underground, like transport and even entire buildings, as it does aboveground. When I speak about unconsciousness, as a city, Tokyo is a place where one can completely concentrate on the task at hand – whatever that may be; conscious awareness of the city one is in. It has a lot to offer and a 24/7 challenging profile, without trying to be loud. Tokyo is not overwhelming. Maybe it is in Shinjuku, or Shibuya, but in general, I think that Tokyo is a city

that's quite easy to live in. We have a house there; a place to work, cook, exhibit, and have a dialogue. People ride their bikes, write short messages, and listen to music all at the same time. But what are these people doing? Biking? Listening to music? Communicating? That's a condition Tokyo presents to you. It's a state of mind. The city allows for that possibility. It has little hierarchy, in the Western sense of the word. It is constantly changing, and adapts to its reality in an elegant way.

There are no outstanding buildings in Tokyo, no outstanding squares, or other such public spaces. It's a vast carpet – a tapestry, even – with more than thirty million people living within its metropolitan borders. For a large part, its infrastructure occurs in a three-dimensional way, below and above ground; subways, highways, and walkways are all represented. I cannot think of a more three-dimensional city than Tokyo. However, it is only partially composed of high-rises, though not as much as you would expect a city its size to have. It's fascinating. You never know in which direction you are going to go. Neighborhoods grow in a rhizomatic way. It's like a film, but a film without a story.

The unconscious, for me, is where we loose contact with the physical. It's a dreamlike condition. It is where everyone, every individual is free to develop their own reading, their own story, everyday – again and again. A never-ending story. And it's important for architects to be aware of.

Shinjuku
Streams of screaming neon, high pitched shrieking sounds; people, people everywhere—silent and robotic. There's no room, there's no escape—earthquakes yet skyscrapers, it's hot, it's

06:06:45

humid, it's calm, it's still for this is Shinjuku—a business and shopping district in the west of Tokyo and the ultimate, overwhelming experience.

PROMPTER

Speaking of the three-dimensionality of Tokyo – how would you describe Los Angeles?

THE ARCHITECT

Los Angeles is extremely one-layered. In that sense it is a true American city, with one-liners and little depth. It is all about the car, and walking is like fighting a battle against the city. It is not three-dimensional and it is not dense. It is extremely un-metropolitan, and un-dense, sort of like a vast village. Of course, Los Angeles also has many moments for possibilities that could be described as unconscious, but Tokyo is so much more. I always recall the accident that James Dean had in 1955 in his Porsche Speedster, to be related to the vastness and flatness of Los Angeles.

I don't want to come up with criteria for an unconscious condition. Los Angeles is somehow very linear, which doesn't allow for copious amounts of phenomena. Oppositely, Tokyo is so dense and so crowded. There are so many programmatic conditions and informational organizational conditions, all overlapping. You have to look for a moment, to hide and to perceive. When we talk about the unconscious, it's of course a state of mind, and it's not unique to Tokyo. But still, the unconscious seems to be encouraged by that particular city.

PROMPTER

And in the Rhine-Ruhr region… do you experience a similar strong unconscious, undefined

condition? Does the German *Autobahn* trigger an unconscious condition?

THE ARCHITECT

Paul Virilio once wrote about the German *Autobahn*, and described it as something without any hierarchy. If a valley needs to be overcome, the *Autobahn* will function as a bridge, while the overall appearance of the surroundings will remain the same.

'*Speed and Politics* (first published in France, 1977) is the matrix of Virilio's entire work. Building on the works of Morand, Marinetti, and McLuhan, Virilio presents a vision more radically political than that of any of his French contemporaries: speed as the engine of destruction. *Speed and Politics* presents a topological account of the entire history of humanity, honing in on the technological advances made possible through the militarization of society. Paralleling Heidegger's account of technology, Virilio's vision sees speed—not class or wealth—as the primary force shaping

06:11:15

civilization. In this “technical vitalism”, multiple projectiles—inert fortresses and bunkers, the “metabolic bodies” of soldiers, transport vessels, and now information and computer technology—are launched in a permanent assault on the world and on human nature. Written at a lightning-fast pace, Virilio’s landmark book is a split-second, overwhelming look at how humanity’s motivity has shaped the way we function today, and what might come of it.’

THE ARCHITECT

The *Autobahn* in Germany has a cinematic condition. All highways do, but all in a different way. Partly dreaming and partly forced. It reminds me of the films by Jean Luc Godard. *Pierrot le Fou*, for example, has a very simple story; much in the way Tokyo has a simple story. And the technique Godard uses in that movie is as so: he takes a shot, then the same again, and then those two are shown overlapped. Then, he’ll sometimes edit in very short advertisements. You hardly see them, but you can see the imprint of the advertisement in your brain, and you can’t fight it. Godard also uses color in a directive way. Red, yellow, and blue. A woman with a red shirt becomes either a secret love, or the personification of foreshadowed danger. Yellow could stand for the countryside; and blue for heaven or

paradise. This is coding, and you're not always aware of it. But then he also uses texts. He uses quotes, and he uses ready-mades. You can watch a Godard movie and get bored. But you will get a great deal more from it than you might initially think. Godard works with an intellectual montage, whilst Sergei Eisenstein employs an emotional montage. I think that Godard's movies revolve around the unconscious condition. Your story, what you take away from the film, doesn't have to necessarily do with Godard's own story – you are free to dream away. I find that very interesting. Even as we take these editing techniques for granted, today.

'When I began filming, I thought of myself as a painter of space engaged on a quest for time. It never occurred to me that this search would be called "storytelling". My stories start with places, cities, landscapes, and roads. A map is like a screenplay to me.'

—Wim Wenders, *On Film: Essays & Conversations* (London: Faber & Faber, 2001).

PROMPTER

Is the Unconscious City more a place, or a virtual condition?

THE ARCHITECT

The Unconscious City is a condition. It's a recognition; and a thought. It's a process of learning and understanding that our world, with all its new technologies, is changing our thought processes. This is an important unconscious aspect to recognize.

The ways in which we're confronted with these new technologies will challenge the current collective state of mind. Our environment has to adapt. And because of this, it is important to speak about these issues, in order to change the way we produce architecture. The shift will further reveal to us that it's not just the architect who makes buildings in the city. It is a collective force. Likewise, nobody planned that the iPhone would so drastically change the way we communicate. It is a smart product, which people enjoy owning and using. It just happened. It's similar to living in a city. No one tells people to move to cities; people do so on their own. To a certain extent this could be seen as an unconscious decision. It's often that people have to move to cities. Previously, decisions were made consciously, as they were based on rules or tradition. People previously belonged to a certain church or family, and no matter what, you were made to feel guilty if you strayed away. I've experienced these eras. If you didn't go to the church, you had to feel guilty. If you lived in a village or neighborhood your whole live, you had to go to the same butcher every week. It was during times like these that Godard made his movies, and showed the world that the new human being will live in a new, nomadic condition. We are living in a nomadic condition. I live in Berlin, Amsterdam, Maastricht, Zürich, and Tokyo, and Chicago. Every week I am traveling within Europe, and I'm in Asia every second month. As we are able to readily fly to every continent, we should not talk about the Unconscious City, but instead, a world that becomes one big cosmopolis. We are now in a kind of jet-lag-like-condition, all the time. And so we have to take care of our body more than ever before; exercise your body as intently and as intensely as you exercise your brain. In this respect Godard is very important for me, as is Valéry and Pavese. They helped me understand these unconscious phenomena. Ernst Jünger often talked of the *Arbeiter*, who, for a few thousand years, worked for a boss. And everyone accepted that hierarchy, unconsciously. But that is no longer.

PROMPTER

Do you see hierarchy as disappearing in the future?

THE ARCHITECT

As we continue amassing more machines, the worker does not become less important, and has instead become trained to produce with his brain. We can now speak of the brain made in the same manner that we previously spoke of the hand made. A specialist works not only for one person, but also for multiple people, and educates himself during the rest of his time. This condition currently exists. The liberation of the *Arbeiter* was a decisive moment in history. There will always be a hierarchy, but it will get a completely different definition in the years yet to come. Hierarchy is no longer used to denote a top-to-bottom relationship, but a sort of balance. For every individual, there are special places, and they are different, but they can't be put into one particular hierarchy. Everyone belongs to multiple clubs now, parallel to one another. The club-society is a very interesting society. It has replaced the postal-code society. Hierarchy and differences are more important now than ever before, which makes the world very competitive for each individual.

PROMPTER

How can we be part of this change, and therefore influence it?

THE ARCHITECT

Architecture will become a much more strategic discipline. We are on our way out from the existing hierarchical society, which is different in many parts of the world, and we are entering a completely new liberal society, with its own hierarchical format, and we don't know much of anything about it. We have to redefine words like hierarchy and liberal, but also democracy. This new society is not predictable. A few years ago people often said, 'Now, there are computers, so we don't need paper anymore.' But we now use more paper than ever, proving that it's very hard to predict these types of changes. In my opinion, this is because no one is in control.

PROMPTER

In order to work more strategically, do words

such as research, intuition, and *zeitgeist* become more important?

THE ARCHITECT

There will always be something like a *zeitgeist*, a momentum, *nowness*. There's a quote by Joost van den Vondel I like: 'He who knows his time is further than his time.' That sounds easy to do, to know your time, but it's not. We need research, on the one hand, and intuition on the other. We have to think about our time, simply by describing it – we have to challenge it – and by being as precise as possible. Research is only composed of facts; it is rational. We can even count the satellites around the world, and I recently found out there are about 80,000 of them, partially as garbage, in orbit around the Earth. But what interests me more is the idea of who is in control. When you read the newspaper, you see stock exchange data, and next to it the experts write about how it might develop. We live in a time of speculation. We're all on a boat, speculating as to whom the captain is, or where we are drifting toward – that's the current situation the world is in. And on this boat are the occasional geniuses that, every so often, develop something revolutionary.

PROMPTER

Living in a time of speculation, what are your current interests?

THE ARCHITECT

I am interested in utopias, but not in designing them. The time utopias were envisioned most was in the late 1960s. Our time is not one of utopias. It is the time of the now. And in my opinion, now is also a time of insecurity. A time in which big statements are no longer made. No one makes big statements anymore. No one at all. We will soon again; it is time for nowness. We must enter a new era; we must take risks; we lack philosophies, we lack discourse, debate, and dialogue on real challenging topics, without the fear of being called radical.

PROMPTER

Considering the iPhone – do you think a company like Apple makes big statements?

THE ARCHITECT

No. They do not. And that's exactly my point.

The iPhone evolved through technology, which is very rational and does not come from a utopian point of origin. I believe we are living in a time in which there will be a radical shift in the production of industry. There will be a revolution in the next few years within technology, which I call 'the technology of the invisible'. It's very stimulating. Even if I have an iPhone, and I use it, it doesn't give my life direction. I can use it to retrieve information and communicate with others, but it obviously doesn't tell me, yet, where to go in life. It is an input and output device. That's all.

'In correlation with these technologies and cultural revolutions, the utopian thought gains, once again, significance in its attempt to invoke, direct, and shape the development of the future. French philosopher, Raymond Ruyer, even observed a structural similarity between scientific and utopian descriptions of the world in his book, *L'Utopie et les Utopies*—the so called mode uto-

pique. In his understanding, utopian thinking is not so much about society: utopia, as a cultural model of understanding, a unique method of comprehension, which employs imaginary elements, in order to try to grasp the present.'

—Robert Klanten, Lukas Feireiss, eds., *Utopia Forever: Visions of Architecture and Urbanism* (Berlin: Gestalten, 2011).

PROMPTER

Where to go in life and what to do in your so-called free time, without any given frame?

THE ARCHITECT

Who has free time? What about when your phone is switched off and its screen's not in front of you? Is that free time?

PROMPTER

What do you think?

THE ARCHITECT

I think that free time has to be completely reinvented. Previously, free time was your time; taking care of your body and mind; walking, doing sports, and having time to read. There was no TV, and no radio, and certainly no devices. The moment we are disconnected from technology is interesting, and it will require specific skills in order to be disconnected. How far do you have to go? We invented the idea of wellness; we've created artificial conditions in which we do nothing, and we're even willing to pay for it. This condition currently already exists. We are paying others, to let us do nothing.

‘The unconscious mind is still viewed by many psychological scientists as the shadow of a “real” conscious mind, though there now exists substantial evidence that the unconscious is not identifiably less flexible, complex, controlling, deliberative, or action oriented than is its counterpart. This “conscious-centric” bias is due in part to the operational definition within cognitive psychology that equates unconscious with subliminal. We review the evidence challenging this restricted view of the unconscious emerging from contemporary social cognition research, which has traditionally defined the unconscious in terms of its unintentional nature; this research has

06:29:15

demonstrated the existence of several independent unconscious behavioral guidance systems: perceptual, evaluative, and motivational. From this perspective, it is concluded that in both phylogeny and ontogeny, actions of an unconscious mind precede the arrival of a conscious mind—that action precedes reflection.'

—John A. Bargh and Ezequiel Morsella, 'The Unconscious Mind', *Perspectives on Psychological Science* 3, no. 1 (January 2008): 73-79.

THE ARCHITECT

There is no alternative, though I have not invented the Unconscious City. I have only invented a word to capture its spirit. And sometimes, you have to invent a word. Many have before me. I think it will be great, for some, to live in the condition of the Unconscious City. And for others, it won't. In every society there are people who are happy and those who are less happy. The Unconscious City does not have a physical preoccupied existence. It is a condition; a circumstance. In fact, it already exists when one's mindset, is able to be open to it. The issue of consciousness is becoming more and more relevant to society today. But let's first ask ourselves: What is fun? The notion of fun is extremely connected to the epoch that you're living within. People today say, 'I'm going to go shopping, for fun!' It's window-shopping and it is totally hollow, as an activity–without any substance. Is substancelessness fun?

PROMPTER

Why not?

THE ARCHITECT

Shopping will definitely not be a topic in the same way it is now, in the near future, and it will eventually subside. I'm not saying we won't go shopping anymore, but the idea of going shopping for fun, for me, is not an act that's durable enough to last. We have to have products, books, vegetables, etc., which are worth while to look for, to buy, and to use. We spoil our fishes in the ocean; we ruin agriculture with mono-culture; we even produce clothes and electronic products, which are not at all needed. Even in a few years this consuming will be further dictated by monobrands that are only interested in our money. What we saw a few years ago, was that people went to musea to relax. People went to musea and had no interest whatsoever in what was on display. That's a habit not worth continuing. The museum and the theater have always been a feast for the mind, to exercise your brain in a conscious and unconscious manner. Your question about fun and the city, specifically the Unconscious City, is very difficult to answer. I am rather interested in the meaning of the world. When you mention the words fun and city, I have to say that the city is not the place for fun, but there are very fun things in it. Maybe the question is better rephrased as, 'Is being in the city a good thing? Is it comfortable?' The main reason people will continue moving to cities during the next thirty years will be because they're comfortable places to be. They are, perhaps, too comfortable and being destroyed by tourism. Let's look toward Martin Heidegger. He talked about resistance and said, 'If there's too much comfort, there's no resistance, no consciousness.' It could be that the new city is too comfortable, too focused on fun, and too little focused on resistance. Maybe it's so extremely smooth, with only tiny problems to worry about and get angry over, but I believe humans need resistance–as you can only be happy if you can also be sad. The city to come might be extremely rough, and resistance will become a huge factor within it. One has to be able to allow, to permit one's self to choose to live in whatever neighborhood in the world they wish. It's incredibly interesting to question what we, as humans, will do.

1. Passage Territories

I'd like to describe in some detail the experience of passing through different territories of the city... I'll start with walls... These walls functioned much like cell membranes, both porous and resistant. That dual quality of the membrane is, I believe, an important principle for visualizing more modern living urban forms. Whenever we construct a barrier, we have to equally make the barrier porous; the distinction between inside and outside has to be breachable, if not ambiguous. The usual contemporary use of plate-glass for walls doesn't do this; true, on the ground plane you see what's inside the building, but you can't touch, smell, or hear anything within. The plates are usually rigidly fixed so that there is only one, regulated,

‘1. Passage Territories
I’d like to describe in some detail the experience of passing through different territories of the city... I’ll start with walls... These walls functioned much like cell membranes, both porous and resistant. That dual quality of the membrane is, I believe, an important principle for visualizing more modern living urban forms. Whenever we construct a barrier, we have to equally make the barrier porous; the distinction between inside and outside has to be breachable, if not ambiguous. The usual contemporary use of plate-glass for walls doesn’t do this; true, on the ground plane you see what’s inside the building, but you can’t touch, smell, or hear anything within. The plates are usually rigidly fixed so that there is only one, regulated,

06:36:00

entrance within. The result is that nothing much develops on either side of these transparent walls, as in Mies van der Rohe's Seagram Building in New York City or Norman Foster's London City Hall: you have dead space on both sides of the wall; life in the building does accumulate here. By contrast, the nineteenth century architect Louis Sullivan used much more primitive forms of plate glass more flexibly, as invitations to gather, to enter a building or to dwell at its edge; his plate glass panels function as porous walls. This contrast in plate glass design brings out one current failure of imagination in using a modern material so that it has a sociable effect. The idea of a cellular wall, which is both resistant and porous, can be extended from single buildings to the

zones in which the different communities of a city meet.

2. Incomplete Form:
This discussion of walls and borders leads logically to a second systematic characteristic of the open city: incomplete form. Incompleteness may seem the enemy of structure, but this is not the case. The designer needs to create physical forms of a particular sort, "incomplete" in a special way. When we design a street, for instance, so that buildings are set back from a street wall, the space left open in front is not truly public space; instead the building has been withdrawn from the street. We know the practical consequences; people walking on a street tend to avoid these recessed spaces. It's better planning if the building is

zones in which the different communities of a city meet.

2. Incomplete Form:
This discussion of walls and borders leads logically to a second systematic characteristic of the open city: incomplete form. Incompleteness may seem the enemy of structure, but this is not the case. The designer needs to create physical forms of a particular sort, “incomplete” in a special way. When we design a street, for instance, so that buildings are set back from a street wall, the space left open in front is not truly public space; instead the building has been withdrawn from the street. We know the practical consequences; people walking on a street tend to avoid these recessed spaces. It’s better planning if the building is

brought forward, into the context of other buildings; though the building will become part of the urban fabric, some of its volumetric elements will now be incompletely disclosed. There is incompleteness in the perception of what the object is. Incompleteness of form extends to the very context of buildings themselves. In classical Rome, Hadrian's Pantheon co-existed with the less distinguished buildings that surrounded it in the urban fabric, though Hadrian's architects conceived the Pantheon as a self-referential object. We find the same co-existence in many other architectural monuments: St. Paul's in London, Rockefeller Center in New York City, the Maison Arabe in Paris—all great works of architecture which stimulate building around themselves. It's

the fact of that stimulation, rather than the fact the buildings are of lesser quality, which counts in urban terms: the existence of one building sited in such a way that it encourages the growth of other buildings around it. And now the buildings acquire their specifically urban value by their relationship to each other; they become in time incomplete forms if considered alone, by themselves.'

–Richard Sennett, "Boundaries and Urban Neighbourhoods: the Open City," Berlin 2006.

PROMPTER
Considering the relationships between buildings, and your statement that humans need resistance, my following question might sound a bit provocative. Are couples getting married only to have conflict in their lives?

THE ARCHITECT
It's interesting that you ask that, because people today are actually marrying less. It's not fashionable to marry, but I believe the real decline has to do with the fact that people don't want to take on responsibility. Not getting married is easy. It's all about easiness.

PROMPTER
But haven't marriage statistics also gone down

06:45:00

the fact of that stimulation, rather than the fact the buildings are of lesser quality, which counts in urban terms: the existence of one building sited in such a way that it encourages the growth of other buildings around it. And now the buildings acquire their specifically urban value by their relationship to each other; they become in time incomplete forms if considered alone, by themselves.'

—Richard Sennett, *'Housing and Urban Neighborhoods; The Open City'*, Berlin, 2006.

PROMPTER

Considering the relationships between buildings, and your statement that humans need resistance, my following question might sound a bit provocative. Are couples getting married only to have conflict in their lives?

THE ARCHITECT

It's interesting that you ask that, because people today are actually marrying less. It's not fashionable to marry, but I believe the real decline has to do with the fact that people don't want to take on responsibility. Not getting married is easy. It's all about easiness.

PROMPTER

But haven't marriage statistics also gone down

because people no longer feel they need to marry young? Are people today less likely to get married, because they no longer feel they have to?

THE ARCHITECT

I think humans do 'marry', and stay with partners, and children, and do recognize legitimate children of partners. Marriage is more than a very old tradition that's engrained in our culture. We view it as a natural human behavior. Very often, such deeply rooted behaviors encourage the urge for change, or escape.

PROMPTER

Is it consequently significant for our current society to remove the cemetery from the city?

THE ARCHITECT

In many cultures, the ancestors have been buried in the vicinity of the living, and usually in the best spots, too. In Hong Kong, Buenos Aires, Barcelona, Paris, and Cairo – cemeteries have been built to celebrate those who have passed away. The 'Day of the Dead' is not only a way of remembering, but also of celebrating life. Cemeteries were originally built on land that was very well located and thus expensive; on land that nowadays one would prefer to build something on. Nowadays people are afraid of dying; it is no longer part of our culture in the ways that it used to be. People now want to live forever; they long for eternal youth, and deny decay. The idea of escaping is now a very topical one. Escaping from responsibility. Moving. Being nomadic. One can leave. It's possible to change your life, your job, your city, country, culture, your partner, and escape reality in a phenomena that is part of our time in which human migration is more complex than ever before. The word 'responsibility' is very important to us. When one used to live in a society, there were rules to live by. Now it's nearly the opposite; there are no rules, and everyone can, more or less, do whatever they want. At a certain moment the question is: 'In which way you are responsible?' What will be the collective responsibility for those whom are

part of the Cosmopolis? This will be a great challenge for our 'Internet'-society.

PROMPTER
Will being a stranger become a situation
that we'll experience much more in the future?
More than we do now?

THE ARCHITECT
When I started teaching at Columbia in the 1990s, I wrote an article that began with the sentence, 'It's good to be a stranger.' It was also the opening sentence of one of my lectures, to introduce my thoughts to the university. I partially live in Amsterdam, Maastricht, Zürich, Tokyo, and Chicago. Because of my soft Dutch accent, being born in the very southern portion of the Netherlands, people think I'm Belgian. For people in the Netherlands who don't know me, I seem to be a stranger. I'm interested in the phenomena that most people in cities are strangers. Is that good or bad? A stranger is extremely conscious about everything. He's curious and adventurous. I like the position of the stranger. There has to be a moment where you ask yourself: 'What do you do with all this information?' One must be able to recycle it. Being a stranger all the time is a condition that, in my opinion, is not productive. It needs to be a temporary state, since one needs time to contemplate and produce.

"Why do we avert our eyes when we encounter the unaccustomed?" asks Sennett. In answer, he moves between past and present from the assembly hall of Athens to the Palladium Club; from Augustine's City of God to the

06:49:30

part of the cosmopolis? This will be a great challenge for our 'internet'-society.

PROMPTER

Will being a stranger become a situation
that we'll experience much more in the future?
More than we do now?

THE ARCHITECT

When I started teaching at Columbia in the 1990s, I wrote an article that began with the sentence, 'It's good to be a stranger.' It was also the opening sentence of one of my lectures, to introduce my thoughts to the university. I partially live in Amsterdam, Maastricht, Zürich, Tokyo, and Chicago. Because of my soft Dutch accent, being born in the very southern portion of the Netherlands, people think I'm Belgian. For people in the Netherlands who don't know me, I seem to be a stranger. I'm interested in the phenomena that most people in cities are strangers. Is that good or bad? A stranger is extremely conscious about everything. He's curious and adventurous. I like the position of the stranger. There has to be a moment where you ask yourself: 'What do you do with all this information?' One must be able to recycle it. Being a stranger all the time is a condition that, in my opinion, is not productive. It needs to be a temporary state, since one needs time to contemplate and produce.

'"Why do we avert our eyes when we encounter the unaccustomed?" asks Sennett. In answer, he moves between past and present from the assembly hall of Athens to the Palladium Club; from Augustine's *City of God* to the

Turkish baths of the Lower East Side; from eighteenth century English gardens to the housing projects of East Harlem; from Nietzsche's *Birth of Tragedy* to subway graffiti. *The Conscience of the Eye* is an exploration of the politics of vision.'

—Richard Sennett, *The Conscience of the Eye: The Design and Social Life of Cities* (New York: W. W. Norton & Company, 1992).

PROMPTER

What are the possible urban consequences from this development?

THE ARCHITECT

When people no longer live in one place for more than five years, why should they buy a house there? If they don't have children, why should they have a house that's designed for a family with them? The condition of ownership, programmatically, is extremely relevant. When buildings and interiors are built in cities–who will occupy them? And for what? And for how long? In Germany the *Bebauungsplan*, in most cases, mainly decides what function a building can have in a certain area. In Japan it's completely different; there is only a zoning law. That's the Japanese way of building. Another consequence could be the possibility of nomadic rules. Where are you paying tax? Maybe in next century the resident tax will no longer be relevant. Imagine you don't spend more than ninety days in any one city. I am interested in these notions: the idea of tax, of ownership, of whom one is building for. It's all about the redefinition of words. We very often give new meanings to words, and we need to be conscious of this.

PROMPTER

There are several levels of communication. One is spoken word, with the common understanding of the words you speak. Then there is the second, the redefinition of words, which communicates through connotation. Another is the ability to enter a dialogue by the way we dress ourselves...

THE ARCHITECT

Gottfried Keller said *Kleider Machen Leute* is about behavior and the way we dress, which in turn tells something about every one of us. When Coco Chanel, who became one of the one of the most influential women of her time, decided to cut her hair and dress like a man, her unconventional appearance changed the way she was perceived, and set a precedent for her statement-making fashion. This, for me, has to do with language. And it also has to do with my interest in the Maasai. They paint their bodies, and use them to communicate, and they ultimately show the condition they're currently in, externally. I like fashion very much. Though I'm not interested in the fashion of seasons, the fashion of trends. Rather, I'm fascinated by the subtle language of fashion, and what it can tell about people and their way of communicating with the world around them. What the Maasai do is a very early human way of expressing oneself, without words, without outspoken language. They are branding themselves with their bodies.

PROMPTER

How is this language connected with the expectations we have for our surroundings? How do we use this to communicate?

THE ARCHITECT

If you go to a restaurant, to the opera, or other public events, and are not dressed the way you are expected to be, people might wonder if you have no understanding of their codes. The world is all about coding and decoding. Sometimes you might have

PROMPTER

There are several levels of communication. One is spoken word, with the common understanding of the words you speak. Then there is the second, the redefinition of words, which communicates through connotation. Another is the ability to enter a dialogue by the way we dress ourselves...

THE ARCHITECT

Gottfried Keller said *Kleider Machen Leute* is about behavior and the way we dress, which in turn tells something about every one of us. When Coco Chanel, who became one of the one of the most influential women of her time, decided, to cut her hair and dress like a man, her unconventional appearance changed the way she was perceived, and set a precedent for her statement-making fashion. This, for me, has to do with language. And it also has to do with my interest in the Maasai. They paint their bodies, and use them to communicate, and they ultimately show the condition they're currently in, externally. I like fashion, very much. Though I'm not interested in the fashion of seasons, the fashion of trends. Rather, I'm fascinated by the subtle language of fashion, and what it can tell about people and their way of communicating with the world around them. What the Maasai do is a very early human way of expressing oneself, without words, without outspoken language. They are branding themselves with their bodies.

PROMPTER

How is this language connected with the expectations we have for our surroundings? How do we use this to communicate?

THE ARCHITECT

If you go to a restaurant, to the opera, or other public events, and are not dressed the way you are expected to be, people might wonder if you have no understanding of their codes. The world is all about coding and decoding. Sometimes you might have

to change clothes three times a day, just because you're confronted with different circumstances. Either you follow the rules, or you don't – but you always express something with that decision. Thomas Mann talks a great deal about non-verbal communication, and I believe the choices we make are a way of telegraphing our values and status to others by, for instance, which glasses you wear, which car you drive, which color that car has, and so on. In one of my lectures there is a photo of Daniel Craig as James Bond; the way he's been photographed makes him appear as a leopard. His nose, his mouth, and his hair – everything contributes to the expression of a strong person; at least, what I consider strong. It is a photo that attempts to communicate how we should see this person. It's a projection, which others can themselves project into upon observing, if it appeals to them. This is part of glamour's appeal; it seduces.

Clothes express what groups one belongs to. And they define borders, also. A Geiko and Maiko, for instance, assume their identities through the way they dress, and only a few others will understand their code of dressing. Hierarchy has changed over time and people have to begin creating their own identities, groups, and codes, which will become more pronounced in the next decades. I think within the next decades of decoding and coding. I think it's being seen as more and more important to create your own identity. Think of Facebook, or Instagram – which I am not part of – they're all about identity. We are living in a self-society. However, this society will develop its hierarchies and rules over time.

PROMPTER

I find it interesting when you speak about hierarchy, or the idea of having no hierarchy, in the future. Or at least, less hierarchy. Hierarchies work with strategies, and as architects we should be interested in working with these strategies. This I find very powerful. If there will, indeed, be less hierarchy in the future, or a shift within that existing system, what will be the role of leaders? What will make someone a leader?

THE ARCHITECT
In the Old World cities had one center, and they were developed from a precedent, with a board, a director, and a speaker. Today we are living in an interbellum. In the future I believe that these organizational structures will change; In the future I believe these organizational structures will be much more flat, more equal. I don't say that there will be no leaders, but I do think it will be less evident that someone will be a leader simply because of their 'power.' He or she will be a leader because of their knowledge. That's a good thing. Tinger said that the *Arbeiter* will be someone not only working with his hands, but also with his mind. When not working, he devotes his time to developing his knowledge. I believe that leaders will continue to become younger and younger. To a certain extent, of course, hierarchy will always be present; the word's connotation, however, is shifting.

It's very romantic to pretend hierarchy should be abandoned, like a century ago in Russia. They had the idea they could develop a society in which everyone is equal and no money exists–a complete socialist, communist idea of equality. It was a time when the linear city was developed. Everyone was supposed to be equal; if a family had a child, it belonged to everyone. Every mother is a model. It lasted for a very short time and was an interesting experiment.

PROMPTER
Would you consider yourself as belonging to a certain group, by wearing Comme des Garçons?

THE ARCHITECT
Because Japanese fashion attempts to liberate, it therefore bridges the gap between men and women, the formal and the informal. Comme des Garçons–a Japanese fashion label founded by Rei Kawakubo, in 1973–does all that for me, and from what I've experienced over the years, I can wear a shirt from them that I bought five years ago, with a jacket I bought yesterday. Although based in Tokyo, they have concept stores, such as since 2005, their market-based department store concept, called Dover Street

06:58:30

THE ARCHITECT

In the Old World cities had one center, and they were developed from a precedent, with a board, a director, and a speaker. Today we are living in an interbellum. In the future I believe that these organizational structures will change. In the future I believe these organizational structures will be much more flat, more equal. I don't say that there will be no leaders, but I do think it will be less evident that someone will be a leader simply because of their 'power'. He or she will be a leader because of their knowledge. That's a good thing. Jünger said that the *Arbeiter* will be someone not only working with his hands, but also with his mind. When not working, he devotes his time to developing his knowledge. I believe that leaders will continue to become younger and younger. To a certain extent, of course, hierarchy will always be present; the word's connotation, however, is shifting.

It's very romantic to pretend hierarchy should be abandoned, like a century ago in Russia. They had the idea they could develop a society in which everyone is equal, and no money exists – a complete socialist, communist idea of equality. It was a time when the linear city was developed. Everyone was supposed to be equal; if a family had a child, it belonged to everyone. Every mother is a model. It lasted for a very short time and was an interesting experiment.

PROMPTER

Would you consider yourself as belonging to a certain group, by wearing Comme des Garçons?

THE ARCHITECT

Because Japanese fashion attempts to liberate, it therefore bridges the gap between men and women, the formal and the informal. Comme des Garçons – a Japanese fashion label founded by Rei Kawakubo, in 1973 – does all that for me, and from what I've experienced over the years, I can wear a shirt from them that I bought five years ago, with a jacket I bought yesterday. Although based in Tokyo, they have concept stores, such as since 2005, their market-based department store concept, called Dover Street

Market. Another just opened in Singapore. They sell there both their own collections, and a wide range of international designers, all under one roof. Comme des Garçons also utilizes the idea of the pop-up shop. It's a pop-up generation, today. But perhaps temporary is a better word. There's a shop in an office, or in a warehouse. It's the idea of being part of a group, going out with friends, and then being invited somewhere else later in the evening, and then another, and so on. The idea of a pop-up shop, is that the customer finds it, but only because they're part of a certain group, or club. People who do not know Comme des Garçons usually say something like, 'You're wearing an interesting shirt.' This is not because it's as identifiable as Chanel, where one immediately sees who made it. I wear the brand because I like it. I don't want to express something, like I would want if I had worn Chanel or Gucci. Yet at the same time, by wearing it, I am indeed expressing something but what? It's the same with a Porsche 911. There is no reason to change that car. It's the same as the 356 that was built in 1948. That's many years ago and the car still has the same flavor. Even though every part has been completely redesigned, there is still a constant message; that of high-quality, elegance, safety, and sophistication – it's a small, perfect car. It's a car for the individual. It's a car that doesn't pretend to be fashionable. You do not see in which year the car was built. That's only possible if you're a specialist. That absence of recognition is what I like about Comme des Garçons, and Porsche.

That is how I feel about my work. I don't want to be fashionable in my work; I want it to work in the long run. I want my buildings to be resistant; they should be more than a shelter – I challenge them. Driving a 911 is not easy. It's difficult. For people who have never driven a 911, it can be dangerous, because the car drives in a different manner than most. Maybe that's what people think, and feel, when they first step inside one of my buildings – a kind of resistance. Though once it is understood, many never want to leave. Comme des Garçons and 911 are very close to the way I strive to develop my work. I think it's quite natural to confront yourself with the things you have a relationship to. Within a recent exhibition of my work there was a portion called the 'Dictionary'.

It was filled with a series of photos and texts, side by side, of, for instance, a picture of the first Porsche or designs by Rei Kawakubo – images that intrigue me. One photo was by Robert Mapplethorpe, whose work I have followed since I first saw it in 1997, in Gallerie Jurka in Amsterdam. I strongly appreciate his attitude of living his ideas. I know it seems dangerous, to show your preferences in such a visual way, but that's what I chose do. I am driven by what I do, and I only do what I love.

PROMPTER

What color is your car?

THE ARCHITECT

It's silver. To me, Porsche is silver. Mine is GT-silver. I asked myself, 'Why should I be fashionable and buy a green or blue or purple Porsche?' If I bought a Ferrari, I would buy it in red. It might not sound exciting to some, but for me it is exciting enough. And that's why I have a silver Porsche.

PROMPTER

With a black interior?

THE ARCHITECT

Yes. Although it should be red leather.

PROMPTER

Do you have a two-wheel or a four-wheel drive?

THE ARCHITECT

Four.

PROMPTER

I would think the two-wheel drive would be even more... classic.

THE ARCHITECT

I have a silver Carrera two-wheel drive, with a manual gear. And that's what's interesting about Porsche; they constantly

research, design, and create new developments. I recently drive, after fifteen years, a GT silver 911 Carrera 4S with automatic gear.

PROMPTER

So this fantastic Porsche 911, four-wheel drive, with cocoa-brown interior, suits you very well.

THE ARCHITECT

That's what's great about Porsche. It's possible to choose the safest car that belongs to this moment in time, while still owning the original Porsche spirit. And there it is: the word ownership. In that sense, I am extremely conscious about the products I buy. If buy a Porsche, why should I buy a car of another make? Why should I have another phone besides the iPhone? Why should I buy anything but Comme des Garçons? I've been buying Comme des Garçons for twenty-five years now, and I have never thrown one shirt away. I don't buy clothes very often. Everything I buy from Comme des Garçons, fits. That's what's interesting about Comme des Garçons; it's easy to understand, and it just works. Like Apple. These are decisions I've made, which associate me with certain groups, and the quality these groups collectively possess. But at the same time, my curriculum vitae is also a reflection of the decisions I've made. For instance, I chose to live in Maastricht, Amsterdam, Zürich, Tokyo, and Chicago. They just happened.

PROMPTER

Do you consider these choice-making possibilities as part of your success?

THE ARCHITECT

I lectured in Glasgow in 2010, and while there a student asked me how success works. 'What can I do?', he asked. But I've never been after success; I'm not interested in success. It can be defined in so many ways. I think people can be very short-minded. Some people are famous today, and tomorrow no one knows them. I define success as being happy with all the things I am doing, at that moment in time. I am able to give shape to my life.

I have a rhythm in my life, which I control. That's success, to me; a way of life that I've determined. The Porsche 911 does not define success. To some it does; but not to me. I could be happy without it. When I lived in Eindhoven, I shared a floor with other students. Yet even there I considered myself very successful, and I was extremely happy, too. I wrote my first book in Eindhoven, and I gave my first lecture there as well. That was a great time in my life. I was happy, and I could work for sixty hours preparing just one lecture. That made me happy. I feel like every day should be holiday. Every time I arrive at an airport, I enter my home, or my office; I should feel such satisfaction of being productive. That's why, I'm a happy man.

07:09:45

専用
路線バス
通学通園バス
通勤送迎バス
日曜 休日を除く
7.30 − 9
DMM
FX

07:12:00

専用
路線バス
通学通園バス
通勤送迎バス
日曜·休日を除く
7.30 − 9
Being Group
DMM
FX

brother

ING

夢
二人で
もう少し
和菓子
作りを
清光 八十才
和子 七十八才
さくら茶
三百円
小袋四季
三百八十
12

07:12:00 –
08:24:00

URBANIZATION

THE PROCESS BY WHICH PEOPLE RESETTLE TO LIVE IN URBAN AREAS.

07:12:00 –
08:24:00

URBANIZATION

THE PROCESS BY WHICH PEOPLE RESETTLE TO LIVE IN URBAN AREAS.

07:14:15

PROMPTER

You had a discourse with Adolf Krischanitz about architecture and urbanism, at the Berlin University of the Arts, during your time as a professor there. Would you like to add anything to that discussion? I am especially interested in knowing how you believe that the two disciplines of architecture and urbanism will develop. What do you think their relation with each other will be, and how do we perceive this relationship?

THE ARCHITECT

When I speak about the word interiority, for me, the word is an idea. People perceive aspects of life because they have senses. Our senses are our skin, our ears, our nose, and our eyes. I believe that one can only sense certain things, and only be aware of certain things, when emotion is also included. When we talk about emotion, or when we talk about perception, we should remember that perception involves the whole body. That's why I'm so interested in Sergei Eisenstein. His films are emotional montages; such an assemblage is today referred to as 'Soviet Montage Theory'. Godard's movies are intellectual montages; the color, the sound...

'Literary criticism stands under the aegis of an inside/outside metaphor that is never being seriously questioned.'
—Paul de Man

'Interiority/Exteriority: Rethinking Emotions, Rüdiger

07:16:30

Campe, Julia Weber, Brigitte Weingart, Yale University: Abstract—'The emergence of the notion of interiority is a modern phenomenon. From antiquity to early modernity, affects or passions were mostly conceived of as external physiological forces, which act upon a passive subject, or as dramatic situations in which the affected person responds to an ensemble of actors and specific circumstances. It is only at the turn of the eighteenth century that emotions became increasingly located within the subject itself. Together with thoughts and ideas they began to form what in German is understood as the *Innenwelt* ("innerworld" or "interiority") of a person. The new distinction between "interiority" and "exteriority" indicates fundamental epistemological and

social transformations. Drawing on Descartes' philosophical distinction between *res cogitans* and *res extensa*, this can also be understood as a consequence of a functional differentiation of society, which, according to sociologist Niklas Luhmann, "slowly took over the place of the former distinction between above and below." Unlike most previous research discussion, which—especially in the German tradition—often focused exclusively on the rise of the modern (romantic) interiority without paying attention to the underlying dichotomy, this conference aims to explore the historical preconditions, the internal logic and the possible shortcomings that inform this discourse. By exploring the genealogy and various manifestations of the opposition "interiority/exteri-

social transformations. Drawing on Descartes' philosophical distinction between *res cogitans* and *res extensa*, this can also be understood as a consequence of a functional differentiation of society, which, according to sociologist Niklas Luhmann, "slowly took over the place of the former distinction between above and below." Unlike most previous research discussion, which—especially in the German tradition—often focused exclusively on the rise of the modern (romantic) interiority without paying attention to the underlying dichotomy, this conference aims to explore the historical preconditions, the internal logic and the possible shortcomings that inform this discourse. By exploring the genealogy and various manifestations of the opposition "interiority/exteri-

ority" we aim to provoke a critical rethinking of the dichotomy and to try out alternative descriptions and analyses.'

—International Conference, Department of German, Whitney Humanities Center, Yale University, New Haven, Connecticut, USA, February, 12-13, 2010.

'The number of different stimuli increases tremendously with the technical development of film. Color and stereoscopic effect, touch, smell, and taste can be activated; the senses can enter into communication with each other. Film can develop into a synthesis of all arts and senses, transcending Richard Wagner's conception of the *Gesamtkunstwerk*. Eisenstein's task consists in delineating these unconsciously perceived moments, in translating units of perception into the level of cognition, and even in finding a mathematical expression for them... The universal law, which

earlier Eisenstein simply labeled “dialectics”, requires now a reinterpretation, a modification for art. The dialectic is now decoded as the feeling that arises through the perception of the image. The path from the level of representation to that of the image involves a semantic conceptualization which includes the sensual perception that Eisenstein defined as ecstasy.’

—Albert J. LaValley and Barry P. Scherr, *Eisenstein at 100: A Reconsideration* (New Brunswick: Rutgers University Press, 2001), 44-45.

THE ARCHITECT

I very strongly believe that the moment we as architects talk about architecture or urbanism, as a concept or strategy where we as architects try to – like a film director makes certain rules, or certain things happen: that is the essence of architecture. If one looks to Malaparte’s villa on Capri – and, I should say, I had the opportunity to stay at the house, for ten days to study it, in early October 1987 – it seems that Malaparte ‘designed the scenery’ himself, as he mentioned to Rommel when he visited the house. To construct the context for the villa could be seen as a strategic urban invention. Situated on the summit of Punta Massulo and surrounded by the sheer cliff of Matromania and the three gigantic rocks of Faragloni, the ‘casa come me’ becomes a violent scene of alienation. Looking through the villa’s fireplace, with its glass-framed background, it becomes a beacon for the fisherman on the rough sea; it is a highly dramatic confrontation between nature and artifice, attraction and repulsion. Architecture and ur-

banism are violent acts of cutting into the existing landscape and creating orientation and disorientation. Both acts I call, 'interiority'. The reason why I am interested in Louis Barragán is because he was a landscape architect that looked toward a site in an incredibly meticulous manner. A wall he would erect as an act to capture nature, and with that incision, or cut, he began to make natural landscapes into artificial ones. The moment he put a roof on top of one of his landscapes, it became an interior. And the moment he added a stair and furniture, it became a room that one could, if desired, call a bedroom. But for me this act of making space is more about the scenario, whether an architect, an urban designer, a stage designer, or gardener. Barragán recognized the circumstances by which we, with our senses, perceive.

PROMPTER

You described your interest in, and inspiration from, film directors like Godard or Eisenstein. Could you draw similar parallels to your way of understanding and creating architecture by collaborating with other professions?

THE ARCHITECT

I make no distinctions between the way I would work as a director and/or an architect. For both, when producing, they develop their ideas as they go along the road. A film director creates a shot, or captures a scene, a movement, which he organized. He can capture this; he can repeat that. And he can do this until it's exactly the way he wants it. In architecture, architects create static interventions in particular landscapes, and they must be aware of how light will enter, how people will move, etc... This is extremely difficult because you're not in control. When you leave, things will happen. An artist can finish his or her piece, but no one can change anything about it after it's considered complete. You can hang art on a wall, put it somewhere; you like it or dislike it. Either way, it's a finished product. A film is the same, to be seen through another medium, a projection in a cinema, a monitor in an airplane – it needs another device. A film is a finished product. The difference is, perhaps, where you watch the

film, or whether you only see a part of it and not the whole. Duchamp once spoke about an artwork's energeia. He said that every piece of art, every architectural piece, has a particular energy. It could be that something is loaded with a particular energy, and that its energy could disappear. It's also possible that some pieces of art have a certain type of energy, but gradually this energy becomes less and less – it disappears. And then, maybe it returns.

During the Rijksmuseum's 'Late Rembrandt' exhibition, I was completely thrilled by a work of his on display. A couple of weeks later, I saw the same work again, and still felt the same strong fascination for it. It was produced in 1631, the year Rembrandt moved from Leiden to Amsterdam, which was exactly the moment he started his studio. And in that phase, you see that his works are so extremely strong. This particular piece is not a painting; it's an engraving of what we call – maybe of his father – an old man. The way he carved into the plate and the way the incision, the track on paper became the black line when printed in ink, creates this incredible tension, and the shadows are so intriguing. For me, back to Duchamp, it still has an incredibly strong energeia.

PROMPTER

Your powerful description of the carved plate that Rembrandt used to make prints, reminds me of your description of urbanism and architecture, specifically, seeing it as 'a cut into the skin of the Earth'.

THE ARCHITECT

Everyone's perception of architecture and urbanism is very important; it has everything to do with our state of mind. What knowledge do we have, collectively and individually? We perceive because of our knowledge. It could be that a particular rock on Lanzarote has been there for three million years, but then at any moment, someone in 2085 could pass by, and cause that to change. Maybe there were people, 1,000 years ago, who passed the same rock. But it's because of our knowledge that we

all perceive the world in different ways. The idea of history really does exist. History is nothing but a story, repeatedly told every day, again and again although always in a different way. Yet it's something we believe in. A kind of religion. History is only considered true because people tell us it is. No one knows exactly what happened ten, a hundred, or even 5,000 years ago. It's just that these stories are repeated, over and over. That's why we believe something happened in the year 0 – which is a pivoting moment, like 0 C, or below and above ground. History is being created everyday, and every second it can change, because of that. History *documents* what was.

PROMPTER

Does that mean architecture leaves a mark on its context, but the individual perception and evolution of it depends on our individual and collective knowledge?

THE ARCHITECT

That's exactly what I believe about architecture and urbanism. It's our task as architects to create incisions in the landscape, whether it's within nature or the city; to create interventions with the knowledge that we have at this very moment. The people who are confronted with these interventions will perceive them through their knowledge. And that's also why one person sees a piece of art differently from the next, and why everyone discovers things differently while watching a film. To a similar extent, everyone has a different perception of a building or an urban intervention, because everyone has a different mindset, and everyone has a different bank of knowledge culled throughout his or her life. Many millions of interventions have been into the Earth over thousands of years; bridges, houses, walls, etc., of which only a very tiny portion of them are designed by architects, who have all the belief that they make the differences. From the pyramids in Egypt to a house in Spain. All are interventions in a certain time and climate. And now that we have started to build beyond Earth, in orbit – which is not the best of conditions for human beings to be in. Humans are always pushing their limit,

looking for challenges, taking risks, and changing our natural habitats. Knowledge is something that's essential to everything I do. Every choice I make about a movement in a building; the way light enters; the way we use a material; how a section works.

All these decisions contribute to the completion of a building are taken within this concept of interiority. My mind; your mind; what is here. This is interiority. Out there – what we call reality – is actually fiction. The moment one dies, reality no longer exists for that individual. At least, that is what it seems to be. That's one of the reasons why so many, over the last 1,000 and 10,000 years, have tried to create a 'God', because the concept of a 'God' is so immense and interesting, and we have no clue who we are, what we are, how we perceive, or where we came from. Since we have a voice, and a written and spoken language, we are able to use words, to change these words, and pronounce these words differently, in many different languages. I think that's extremely important for architects to remember, because no one sees the same thing in the same way, ever. A good building one sees and experiences differently during each visit. It's the same with words.

PROMPTER

Do I remember correctly that you had a special preference for the Webster's dictionary as a student?

THE ARCHITECT

When you look at a Webster's dictionary, and look up a word, it often has different meanings. This layering of connotations, this layering of stories, is what makes our lives so interesting. And that's also what I mean when I speak about 'history', which we could potentially change. This is what makes me so positive about the present, and what I'm currently doing. I believe that the moment we have to deal with architecture and urbanism, we must be aware of the time we are living within. I think in terms of teaching yourself, as an ongoing process of reflection and gained knowledge. This is most important. It is a process of selec-

looking for challenges, taking risks, and changing our natural habitats. Knowledge is something that's essential to everything I do. Every choice I make about a movement in a building; the way light enters; the way we use a material; how a section works.

All these decisions contribute to the completion of a building are taken within this concept of interiority. My mind; your mind; what is here. This is interiority. Out there – what we call reality – is actually fiction. The moment one dies, reality no longer exists for that individual. At least, that is what it seems to be. That's one of the reasons why so many, over the last 1,000 and 10,000 years, have tried to create a 'God', because the concept of a 'God' is so immense and interesting, and we have no clue who we are, what we are, how we perceive, or where we came from. Since we have a voice, and a written and spoken language, we are able to use words, to change these words, and pronounce these words differently, in many different languages. I think that's extremely important for architects to remember, because no one sees the same thing in the same way, ever. A good building one sees and experiences differently during each visit. It's the same with words.

PROMPTER

Do I remember correctly that you had a special preference for the Webster's dictionary as a student?

THE ARCHITECT

When you look at a Webster's dictionary, and look up a word, it often has different meanings. This layering of connotations, this layering of stories, is what makes our lives so interesting. And that's also what I mean when I speak about 'history', which we could potentially change. This is what makes me so positive about the present, and what I'm currently doing. I believe that the moment we have to deal with architecture and urbanism, we must be aware of the time we are living within. I think in terms of teaching yourself, as an ongoing process of reflection and gained knowledge. This is most important. It is a process of selec-

tion, making choices, reading a text as if you were holding it up to a mirror. It reminds both student and professor to be aware of time. I, as a professor and dean, cannot teach by saying that *this* is the way it should be done. I can only tell students that they should educate themselves, that they should research, define and know which time they are living in, and understand it so that they can react to it. Everyone can learn from each construct, built in whatever time and on whatever site, when one has eyes that want to see. One must be curious, interested, and ready to formulate what it is that one sees, and thinks about it.

PROMPTER

What does that mean for your interaction with clients, and in particular, those who do not have an architectural background?

THE ARCHITECT

When I have a dialogue with someone, perhaps someone who asked me to design a project or product for them, I have to create a certain degree of knowledge. I can only attempt to educate them, drink a small bit, in architecture. Before we can begin to talk about an intervention, I have to let the other person know that architecture has more concerns than just the façade or the style – and that it must reflect the time we live in. But at the same time, I have to formulate the other's question. I have to talk with them, eat with them, drink with them – all to understand who they are, and what their mindset is – and more importantly, could be! I must first know this. While doing all this, I must also explain to the client what my views on architecture and urbanism are. To be a client is extremely difficult. It follows the same principle of being a parent. When you have a child, you have no clue what to do with it, at first. I had this experience when my daughter was born, and also my son. It's an odd sensation. Yet it's very often the case that people are not educated on how to be parents. You must discover this for yourself. And it's the same with my students, my friends, and the same with my clients.

PROMPTER

Is that where urbanism comes into play?

THE ARCHITECT

When working with a particular site, there will often be a neighbor, a context in which to work, and often times there was something there, on the site, before. The intervention as such is changing it, adding a new potential to it, a strongly formulated strategic device. This sensibility is extremely important to an architect. I think at the moment an architect's work is done, and they have completed a building, they have made an intervention in the city, which could be organized as a positive virus. When I've made an intervention in a city, I go back to it, quite often.

PROMPTER

You are saying that the effect or what you have done to the urban context is something, which becomes visible or noticeable after completing the building. Would you agree that, although through its realization, the first part of the job is done; there are still many important steps that follow? These steps often deal with the real interaction, with its context, and the acceptance of the interior.

THE ARCHITECT

I once had a meeting with the then new director of the Utrecht University Library. He invited me for a lecture, so that I could do two things at once: I walked around to see how the building has changed, and also to see how the building has been accepted. Architecture, urbanism, and interior design are, for me, all part of the same profession. Like Adolf Loos, I design spoons, and cities. Even when speaking about engineering – installations, electronics, heating, or cooling – it's almost always part of an architectural intervention. If a building has a particular acoustic aura, the perception of that building will be different from one moment to another. Architects must very carefully test the acoustics of their buildings. I'm very much interested in conditioning systems.

I only want to have radiant heating or cooling in buildings I design, because they're the most natural systems, for instance. And the way the light enters a space; I'm extremely sensible to that. Because light is extremely aggressive when there is a façade with light entering directly through it. That's aggressive. How do I take care that, when it's raining, the clouds still create a completely different light in a room than it would if the sun were shining? How the floor is made, not only the stone and the color, but also the sound it makes when walked on. That's all an architectural intervention; that's all part of architecture. For instance, when I walk through Venice in the very early morning, after midnight, and there's no one on the street, no one on the narrow bridges, with a soft yellow light surrounding me, with some patches of color, and I walk, and I hear my own footsteps echoing... That's architecture. That's urbanism. That's all part of my sensibility.

PROMPTER

As all our senses are challenged through architecture: which role does technology play within that stimulating experience?

THE ARCHITECT

Technology must be incorporated within buildings, as well. And architecture develops partially because of the development of technology. That's why Gothic Cathedrals could be realized. They were the result of technological innovation. They were realized with a collective effort, which belonged to their time. With the iPhone and other devices, as smartphones, I can – for instance – control the inner-workings of my house from 1,000 km away, from anywhere. I can look into my house, because there's a camera. I can control my heating and cooling systems. And, I can use my iPhone as the key to enter my house. The iPhone is the apparatus. But it doesn't replace the sensual experiences we can create through architecture. So, what I'm trying to say is: know what is possible at this moment, decide if you think it's worthwhile, and if so, use it! This new technology for our houses, which enables us to control so many aspects of it when not at home, is something I'm extremely aware of and extremely interested in. It

makes the perception of the people who use that house much stronger. It's all part of the way we perceive. It's strange that cities are not making use of new technologies, to manipulate how buildings can interact: how the street and the neighborhood become a bigger interface. Or maybe they already are, and we are just unconscious about it. When you go to a party, you believe to know something about the party before you enter the door. Before you have even arrived and shaken hands with guests, you'll immediately have an intuitive feeling about whether this will be a good night or not. The manipulation of perception, or the orchestration of perception, has everything to do with a choreographer's development of movement. The concept of the choreographer, who tries to transfer a certain moment to the audience, what he captures, and what is perceived while sitting in the theater is something that we - as architects - should be much more aware of. When entering a house, I always want it to feel like a challenge, like a feast for the mind. What stage sets are we creating for the inhabitants of the building we craft?

PROMPTER

There was an article in the *Atlantic* that raised the question: 'Are our minds being altered due to our increasing reliance on search engines, social networking sites, and other digital technologies?'

'Over the past few years, I've had an uncomfortable sense that someone, or something, has been tinkering with my brain, re-mapping the neural circuitry, reprogramming the memory. My mind isn't going—so far as I can tell—but it's changing. I'm

07:43:30

makes the perception of the people who use that house much stronger. It's all part of the way we perceive. It's strange that cities are not making use of new technologies, to manipulate how buildings can interact; how the street and the neighborhood become a bigger interface. Or maybe they already are, and we are just unconscious about it. When you go to a party, you believe to know something about the party before you enter the door. Before you have even arrived and shaken hands with guests, you'll immediately have an intuitive feeling about whether this will be a good night, or not. The manipulation of perception, or the orchestration of perception, has everything to do with a choreographer's development of movement. The concept of the choreographer, who tries to transfer a certain moment to the audience, what he captures, and what is perceived while sitting in the theater, is something that we – as architects – should be much more aware of. When entering a house, I always want it to feel like a challenge, like a feast for the mind. What stage sets are we creating for the inhabitants of the building we craft?

PROMPTER

There was an article in the *Atlantic* that raised the question: 'Are our minds being altered due to our increasing reliance on search engines, social networking sites, and other digital technologies?'

'Over the past few years, I've had an uncomfortable sense that someone, or something, has been tinkering with my brain, remapping the neural circuitry, reprogramming the memory. My mind isn't going—so far as I can tell—but it's changing. I'm

07:43:30

not thinking the way I used to think. I can feel it most strongly when I'm reading. Immersing myself in a book or a lengthy article used to be easy. My mind would get caught up in the narrative or the turns of the argument and I'd spend hours strolling through long stretches of prose. That's rarely the case anymore. Now my concentration often starts to drift after two or three pages. I get fidgety, lose the thread, and begin looking for something else to do. I feel as if I'm always dragging my wayward brain back to the text. The deep reading that used to come naturally has become a struggle.'

—Nicholas Carr, 'Is Google Making Us Stupid?: What the Internet is Doing to Our Brains', *Atlantic*, July/August 2008.

PROMPTER

But it is also mentioned in the same article that, 'Not all neuroscientists agree with Carr and some psychologists are skeptical. Harvard's Steven Pinker, for example, is openly dismissive.'

07:45:45

'Critics of new media sometimes use science itself to press their case, citing research that shows how "experience can change the brain". But cognitive neuroscientists roll their eyes at such talk. Yes, every time we learn a fact or skill the wiring of the brain changes; it's not as if the information is stored in the pancreas. But the existence of neural plasticity does not mean the brain is a blob of clay pounded into shape by experience... The new media have caught on for a reason. Knowledge is increasing exponentially; human brainpower and waking hours are not. Fortunately, the internet and information technologies are helping us manage, search, and retrieve our collective intellectual output at different scales, from Twitter and pre-

‘Critics of new media sometimes use science itself to press their case, citing research that shows how “experience can change the brain”. But cognitive neuroscientists roll their eyes at such talk. Yes, every time we learn a fact or skill the wiring of the brain changes; it’s not as if the information is stored in the pancreas. But the existence of neural plasticity does not mean the brain is a blob of clay pounded into shape by experience... The new media have caught on for a reason. Knowledge is increasing exponentially; human brainpower and waking hours are not. Fortunately, the internet and information technologies are helping us manage, search, and retrieve our collective intellectual output at different scales, from Twitter and pre-

07:48:00

views, to e-books and online encyclopedias. Far from making us stupid, these technologies are the only things that will keep us smart.'

—Steven Pinker, 'Mind Over Mass Media', *New York Times*, 10 June, 2010.

PROMPTER

Wiel, when you speak about technology changing our daily routines, how will these routines change?

THE ARCHITECT

It's both fascinating and worrying. For instance, say you're driving home, you're going to your apartment, and your device is with you in your car. When you enter your building, the car park will direct you to the fifth floor, not the fourth, but the fifth – because that's where your parking space is. You then park your car in your spot. Or, perhaps the car will park itself, without your help. Once you've left your car and walked away, the light in the parking garage automatically goes off. You go to the elevator and there's no button, because you don't need one. The elevator knows to take you to the 22nd floor, because that's where you live. You make your way to your front door, and it automatically opens when you arrive. The moment you enter your house, the light goes on. Your home, and your device both know its 9pm, and that you've programmed, perhaps, soft light for the evening. And maybe, the espresso machine is on, because you've decided that morning, that you'd want an espresso then. Your home knows all this. You can program as much as you like, or as little as you like. Yes. All of this is quite interesting, because these types of technology can quite literally tell the building that, for instance, when you leave, it should cool down. Buildings can complete tasks on their own, by which we can save energy. All of this is no longer futuristic for the individual inhabitant of a metro-

polis; instead, it will soon be part of our daily metropolitan routines. However, this all happens outside our mind. So we have to be careful not to overestimate technology. We should develop ourselves and understand that philosophy is still the key discipline from progressive research.

PROMPTER

You spoke before about the manipulation of our perception...

THE ARCHITECT

When you go to the party, or to your friend's house, it's extremely important how this act is orchestrated. When my wife and I were married, in 1991, people were told that the wedding party would take place in a castle on the Dutch-Belgian border, and everyone thought we would have the wedding in the castle. They were partly right. People came from England, France, from all over to attend our wedding party. We had told the owner of the castle that we wanted to have our party in the grotto; essentially a cave that's part of the castle's complex, used as a wine cellar, 16 C and 'rough' as it had been for many centuries. It's a result of the mining done for the stone for the castle, and other buildings realized in the area; it is a maze of tunnels of more than 250 km. He said that that would not be possible. As it was not part of their routine, they perhaps thought the idea was 'below their standards'. I said, 'We'll do it and you don't have to do anything. We'll just put in some candles and a grand piano.' So, on our wedding night, everyone was completely overwhelmed when they were welcomed into this very transcending scenario. By dusk, people had dinner and drinks, and were standing there, in this cave, surrounded by beautiful dimly lit candlelight. It was magical. We were told it was impossible, but we managed to realize it. We created an expectation, which was replaced by a completely different experience. And this metaphor is applicable to architecture in many different ways. Architecture is not just a particular building that one happens to be working on. It's a situation. It's not only a section or plan. Architects must be able to understand how people will, or could, react to their spaces. Disturbances,

polis; instead, it will soon be part of our daily metropolitan routines. However, this all happens outside our mind. So we have to be careful not to overestimate technology. We should develop ourselves and understand that philosophy is still the key discipline from progressive research.

PROMPTER

You spoke before about the manipulation of our perception...

THE ARCHITECT

When you go to the party, or to your friend's house, it's extremely important how this act is orchestrated. When my wife and I were married, in 1991, people were told that the wedding party would take place in a castle on the Dutch-Belgian border, and everyone thought we would have the wedding in the castle. They were partly right. People came from England, France, from all over to attend our wedding party. We had told the owner of the castle that we wanted to have our party in the grotto; essentially a cave that's part of the castle's complex, used as a wine cellar, 16 C and 'rough' as it had been for many centuries. It's a result of the mining done for the stone for the castle, and other buildings realized in the area; it is a maze of tunnels of more than 250 km. He said that that would not be possible. As it was not part of their routine, they perhaps thought the idea was 'below their standards'. I said, 'We'll do it, and you don't have to do anything. We'll just put in some candles and a grand piano.' So, on our wedding night, everyone was completely overwhelmed when they were welcomed into this very transcending scenario. By dusk, people had dinner and drinks, and were standing there, in this cave, surrounded by beautiful dimly lit candlelight. It was magical. We were told it was impossible, but we managed to realize it. We created an expectation, which was replaced by a completely different experience. And this metaphor is applicable to architecture in many different ways. Architecture is not just a particular building that one happens to be working on. It's a situation. It's not only a section or plan. Architects must be able to understand how people will, or could, react to their spaces. Disturbances,

irritation; these words are incredibly important. They're a kind of positive conflict. At the Berlage Institute, I used to use these types of words each year, to shape a sort of theme. And then, the research done that year, for instance, would deal with the word–like conflict. How can we make architecture by thinking about conflict? How can we make architecture by thinking about disturbances? How can we talk about architecture when we deal with forces?

PROMPTER

You stated before that perception is dependent on knowledge, and I would add experience. The word conflict means conflict, for some, but might not it be seen as a conflict, for others?

THE ARCHITECT

Conflict is always, always there. For everything we do, for every single moment, there is a conflicting moment. Because a conflict is not necessarily something negative. Conflict is simply the difference between the way I say something, and the way that another perceives it. Conflict can be resistence. I say something, and your brain perceives something else, and then a conflicting situation could arise. Everyone thinks differently. So no matter what I say, you will always read it differently. I say something; you listen. And we each have something else on our minds, even as we say: 'Yes, yes, yes.' I have something else on my mind right now, than you. For me it's only interesting when we are aware of that. And when you are aware, you can manipulate this. You can use this condition to your benefit. That's why, when I was dean of the Berlage Institute, I used words like: strategic device, progressive research, fields, forces, choice, and conflict. These words communicate a kind of instability. They manifest differences, which are omniscient. The fact that some speak about a state of perfection, is only because perfect is unachievable on Earth. Everything is imperfect. So let us better concentrate on the imperfect condition, and the ways in which this can help us develop. We should be aware that when we do something, as an architect, that many people will end up reading this architecture in many different ways. No one is ever able to make a project

perfect. When we accept imperfection, we can deal with it. I don't believe in perfection; I only believe in imperfection. Only then can one understand, and work with, this notion. Shinohara wrote a fantastic article, 'Tokyo–The Beauty of Chaos'. Tokyo is a city of chaos, and while reading one begins to understand this city more and more. One understands its rules and its constant factors. And this is why I'm so interested in rules. The moment we are able to develop a few key rules, we can develop these rules with freedom in mind. A rule is not non-freedom. A rule does not say that one can't do something else. A rule can be interpreted; a rule will always give freedom. Freedom without rules is impossible. It's the same with what kept me busy when I designed a police station for Vaals, a small city in the south of the Netherlands, near the German border, by Aachen. I had to design prison cells, and when I designed them, I remember very well, that I made a window, which according to the program, was not possible to make about 5 km away, there is a monastery by Hans van Der Laan called Abbey Sint Benedictusberg. In this monastery, monks deliberately spent their time in a cell, and these cells had windows. The monastery and the police station are within visual distance from one another. The prisoners in the police cell are there without consent. Yet I thought it would be interesting to confront the cell of the police station, where the prisoner is against free will, with a monk in his cell, who is there by free will. One person is in a cell by choice, and the other is in a cell with a locked door–and yet they can both see one another. This consideration, kept me quite busy.

PROMPTER

You mentioned Tokyo, and since we are talking about architecture and urbanism, let's talk about icons. How important is the icon for urban discussion? For urbanity? As you say, Tokyo seems to be an iconless city.

THE ARCHITECT

Before I give an answer, could you please tell me what, for you, is an icon? There are many different types. What is it that you're looking for with this question?

PROMPTER

In regards to architecture, an icon is a building with a very high significance.

THE ARCHITECT

Tokyo doesn't have any icons. Maybe for you the icon is a kind of monument, which people talk about, like the Eiffel Tower. Tokyo doesn't have any icons, in that sense. Maybe Mt. Fuji with its white top of snow, will be the only one. But Tokyo does have an incredible amount of other icons. Everywhere in the street there are icons, because people are, for one reason or the other, excited about symbols. Icons have a lot to do with comics. There is no other culture besides that of Japan, where the comic strip is ubiquitous. When you buy a can of sake or beer in Japan, there's usually a comic showing you how to open it. As a foreigner in Japan, you would never think there's sake inside the can. You would just think it's a very sweet children's drink, because the comic itself on the back of the can is extremely childish; at least when seen from a European perspective. There is always a story being told in Japan. Even when you drive, you look to the icon on the street. That is story telling. Japanese are less interested in the form. This is in juxtaposition to, for instance, the French, who are interested in the icon, and the Eiffel Tower; the ultimate expression of form. That's also why you simply must go to Kyoto, or Ryōan-ji, with its fantastic gardens – or, perhaps, Katsura Palace, when you are next in Japan. These places have each created a setting. The moment you go to the Ryōan-ji, and walk barefoot on a 60 cm elevated wooden floor, and sit there, and see the white small stones that look like the sea… it's incredible. People sit on this floor, and they begin to create their own stories. They meditate. In Japanese culture, it's not important whether the outer shape is spectacular, or not. It's more about what a particular moment evokes. That's also why, if you give someone a present in Japan, the wrapping is often more important than the present itself. This is because the wrapping creates a kind of expectation as to what's inside. So the inside of anything, in this respect, as long as you don't see it, is very important, too. It's the same when you go to the Gion district of Kyoto, where Geisha,

about 142 of them, live and work. It's the expectation that enhances the fascination. It's what Geisha evoke, what they could be. When you look at the Eiffel Tower, it's there. It's a spectacular structure built of steel, which has become the symbol of Paris. That's a phenomenon, and that interests me. A lot.

PROMPTER

Could we proceed from the assumption that objects and situations should leave space for individual readings?

THE ARCHITECT

It's these layered meanings that interest me most.

PROMPTER

And how will this change our relationship to the city?

THE ARCHITECT

What we really must realize is that until the turn of this century, relationships between people and a particular city were usually long lasting. People were often born there, educated there, had friends there, and so on. Most people even died there. They knew everything about that place. They knew their families, the city's streets, the baker, and the grocers. But when you think about the fact that we are just nomads, and that nearly everyone in a city is a stranger, you get a completely different awareness of what a city is. It's like wrapping a present. You walk and there is a surprise, and then another. At every moment, everything goes so quickly. Everything becomes a surprise. That's why cities change. Whatever we do as architects, the city will still change. The interesting thing is, however, that when we—as architects—are aware of this factor, we should be conscious that we are not object-makers. We need to deal with architecture in a much more strategic way. And we have to understand that we have become part of a larger global debate. We have to be in contact with decision makers, and be part of their debate. We should take care not to be isolated from the debate about progressiveness,

08:01:30

about 142 of them, live and work. It's the expectation that enhances the fascination. It's what Geisha evoke, what they could be. When you look at the Eiffel Tower, it's there. It's a spectacular structure built of steel, which has become the symbol of Paris. That's a phenomenon, and that interests me. A lot.

PROMPTER

Could we proceed from the assumption that objects and situations should leave space for individual readings?

THE ARCHITECT

It's these layered meanings that interest me most.

PROMPTER

And how will this change our relationship to the city?

THE ARCHITECT

What we really must realize is that until the turn of this century, relationships between people and a particular city were usually long lasting. People were often born there, educated there, had friends there, and so on. Most people even died there. They knew everything about that place. They knew their families, the city's streets, the baker, and the grocers. But when you think about the fact that we are just nomads, and that nearly everyone in a city is a stranger, you get a completely different awareness of what a city is. It's like wrapping a present. You walk, and there is a surprise, and then another. At every moment, everything goes so quickly. Everything becomes a surprise. That's why cities change. Whatever we do as architects; the city will still change. The interesting thing is, however, that when we – as architects – are aware of this factor, we should be conscious that we are not object-makers. We need to deal with architecture in a much more strategic way. And we have to understand that we have become part of a larger global debate. We have to be in contact with decision makers, and be part of their debate. We should take care not to be isolated from the debate about progressiveness,

which is currently happening in all technological fields, all economic fields, and in all medical research. Medical research and technological research, in terms of materials and in terms of new advancements, is not only possible but also necessary for architects to undertake.

PROMPTER

How can we – as architects – be part of that? The change of perception in the history of mankind has always been essential to the change of the urban construct.

THE ARCHITECT

When the Great Pyramids were built in Egypt, they were positioned at the precise millimeter according to a predetermined concept and strategy. It was a very precise act. When, in Athens, the Parthenon was positioned, the entrance and the way in which it could be perceived were all done according to a set strategy. Architectural tools have changed much over millennia. During the times of the pyramids, people believed in eternity, and that the Pharaoh was a 'God'. The Parthenon was constructed based on the relationship between the Greeks, the human body, and religion. It was in Greece that, for the first time, the human body was placed within history. In the Renaissance, perspective was rediscovered as a tool. Hence the developments of the city, and the development of architectural products, have changed dramatically throughout the course of 'history'. There's that word again... When the Industrial Revolution began, architecture changed too. Suddenly, humans were able to erect buildings that were previously impossible. And now with, let's say, the Modern Movement and the Inter-national Style, the introduction of IT, the introduction of movement, the third dimension of the Renaissance, the fourth dimension of speed, and the fifth dimension – thinking that we are able to move with our minds – we are at another extremely interesting moment, where, through technology, the world is again set to change. People are beginning to think differently, and in the future, our cities will reflect this. What I've tried to do is suggest that we have to be aware of the issue or the question: What is

the impact of technology on our minds? How is our unconscious changed? And how can we – as architects – be aware of this, in order to create a new architecture? Le Corbusier understood the machine had an impact on architecture. Leonardo Da Vinci and Michelangelo both challenged the human body, as well as our perception of perspective. What happened in the 1960s? Groups like Archigram had the feeling that we were living in a time of pop culture. And that the Walking City was our domain. Yet we now understand that we can, indeed, dream. But at the same time, the world we live in is very real. Because, in the 1960s, one could easily say things like: 'In thirty years this and this will happen.' But now we know that it's today that matters most, and that when you have an idea, you have to do it now, because if not, tomorrow someone else will do it for you. So the immediacy of how events unfold, is something that everyone should be aware of. However, I myself like the dream like condition.

PROMPTER

Does the Unconscious City describe a strategy that should remain associative to the changes of our time?

THE ARCHITECT

Yes. That's why when we speak about the Unconscious City; we can't say that it will look like *this*. We have to instead attempt to understand what the impact of unconsciousness truly is. Then we must understand what our position is as architects and urban designers? We can only have a position when we have a strategy. When we are advanced, we know our time. That's another reason why I'm so interested in Godard. He understood very well, how to bring a story across; How to connect color and sound; How to bring these different layers, the puppet, the advertisement, the voice; How to bring them all together; How to make a type of collage, to take the viewer, the perceiver, seriously. How to give the title a transparency, a multi-layered meaning, eg. *Pierrot le Fou, Le Mempris, Je vous salue, Marie.*

PROMPTER

But this multi-layering also requires us to accept the liberty of everyone being able to understand a film, a city, or a building differently, according to his or her individual knowledge. This might lead to a different reaction, and thus an individual processing.

THE ARCHITECT

We are living in a time in which everyone is slowly becoming equal, in terms of respect. Even though, individual qualities of one person, can certainly, at least meritocratically, 'surpass' those deemed at the apex of a society's 'accepted' hierarchy. We take everyone seriously and we have to respect their work–hence the blurring of the lines between hierarchies. But we must respect them, and differences. We've reached a point where, eventually, everyone will have equal possibilities. That's doesn't, however, mean that everyone is equal, because everyone does things differently from the next person. There is competition, eagerness. But equality is something that's creating a new city, in which people no longer have the desire to build icons, because there's new ways to connect to others. Again; capital, matters.

PROMPTER

That also relates to the individual processing, which we spoke about before. Our experiences will lead to different chain reactions, all influenced by the variety of possible choices.

THE ARCHITECT

You can be part of a city that's also the world's city. In this idea, the world is one big city and we have neighborhoods that are not just inhabited by people who've lived there their whole lives. That will be, I think, the biggest change and challenge for our cities in the future. People are becoming fluid in their movement from place to place. This nomadic condition is currently having an incredible impact on the world's cities, and on its neighborhoods. I once gave a lecture at the Société Française, in Paris. After

the lecture someone asked: What's the relationship between your work and the text I read in your book? And that's a very interesting question. I can't exactly say, I wrote it like *this*, and built it like *that*. But yet I can say, whether I'm working on a house or a museum or a theater, that I try to be aware of the time I am in, and how I think, at that very moment: How do people perceive things, and how I can react to that condition? That's my task as urban designer. I have to make decisions that will have an imprint for a very long time, and so fashionable is not my cup of tea. That's my task as an architect.

PROMPTER

Since you refer to technology quite often, could you describe what has really changed in our world? What wasn't like it is now, before? Any examples? The question is still: How do we parlay the current change of our minds into our changing architecture, and the perception of that architecture?

THE ARCHITECT

I'm not an architect who is interested in spectacles. But let me first answer your question. What has changed, in the context of these new devices? There are two things: One is that distance is becoming less and less important. I communicate with this device which is a very pragmatic act. I do my emails; I make phone calls; I write text messages; I take photos; I broadcast; I collect and share digital information, wherever I am. All of this, on one apparatus. One apparatus makes my life easier. And that's very pragmatic. The second is what I explained to you before: This apparatus–the iPhone–often connects me to a building I inhabit. Besides what I've already explained, this device can help me easily buy a railway ticket; remind me what I have to do tonight; that I have a flight to catch; that I have to vote. I can also pay with it and, as I explained, I can enter my house with it. These all very pragmatic things that have changed both my consciousness and unconsciousness, and because of this, my relationship to the world has changed too. I am less dependent on the physical

the lecture someone asked: 'What's the relationship between your work, and the text I read in your book?' And that's a very interesting question. I can't exactly say. I wrote it like *this*, and built it like *that*. But yet I can say, whether I'm working on a house or a museum or a theater, that I try to be aware of the time I am in, and how I think, at that very moment. How do people perceive things, and how I can react to that condition? That's my task as urban designer. I have to make decisions that will have an imprint for a very long time, and so fashionable is not my cup of tea. That's my task as an architect.

PROMPTER

Since you refer to technology quite often, could you describe what has really changed in our world? What wasn't like it is now, before? Any examples? The question is still: How do we parlay the current change of our minds into our changing architecture, and the perception of that architecture?

THE ARCHITECT

I'm not an architect who is interested in spectacles. But let me first answer your question. What has changed, in the context of these new devices? There are two things: One is that distance is becoming less and less important. I communicate with this device, which is a very pragmatic act. I do my emails; I make phone calls; I write text messages; I take photos; I broadcast; I collect and share digital information, wherever I am. All of this, on one apparatus. One apparatus makes my life easier. And that's very pragmatic. The second is what I explained to you before: This apparatus–the iPhone–often connects me to a building I inhabit. Besides what I've already explained, this device can help me easily buy a railway ticket; remind me what I have to do tonight; that I have a flight to catch; that I have to vote. I can also pay with it and, as I explained, I can enter my house with it. These all very pragmatic things that have changed both my consciousness and unconsciousness, and because of this, my relationship to the world has changed too. I am less dependent on the physical

location that I am at, at any given moment. Anyone on the globe, at any moment, is accessible for me to connect to.

PROMPTER

How is the globe changing?

THE ARCHITECT

I see the world less and less as a physical thing. Today a surgeon can of course perform an operation from his office in California, on a patient having their surgery in Amsterdam; but that is technology, although it has a large impact on how we think and therefore, continue to develop it. Although, technology is a tool like any other, and we must not overrate it. The real challenge will always be with its content, and so literature and art like philosophy are key progressive disciplines. It's these sorts of things that make you understand that our world is simply different.

PROMPTER

Do certain technologies, such as the iPhone, keep us from discovering the world that's still disconnected to such technologies?

THE ARCHITECT

Ray and Charles Eames made furniture, and they made their house, which they lived in for the rest of their life. But at the same time, they traveled to Africa. They understood that the mindset of the people they met in Africa would be a different one than that of those in America. They didn't say that one was better, or worse. They understood that a mindset was something they could learn. They didn't say: 'We are from America, we undertake material research, we are able to bend wood, we are able to make cars, and therefore we are advanced.' No. They attempted and began to understand the local cultures, the people, to appreciate them more, and to bring them into their advanced world. One thing I would never do, is say that everything I learn about the world through a device like the iPhone, enabling me to see the world in different ways, makes me, for instance, not interested in a particular African tribe. In fact, it's the opposite. My device enables

me to understand them even better, from anywhere. To be more conscious and able to see the richness of what tribes, and the world, have developed is priceless. Even without physically coming in contact with them; I'm able to educate myself on their way of life. That doesn't mean that I'm suddenly able to empathize, or seamlessly merge into their lives. But at least I have educated myself about them; and in the process, increase my empathy toward others. That brings me again to Godard.

In his movies there is usually a collapse. For instance, on the one hand, the collapse of an African tribe. On the other hand, I'm using the most advanced technology to see this collapse. All that information enters my brain, upon which I am conscious and unconsciously connecting events. Situations like these will create, in a very unconscious way, a new piece of architecture. But it's not that I can tell you exactly what that will be, or is. To me, this current technological revolution is overwhelming, and we should not forget to see what is still physically there. We should go to Lanzarote and walk on the island for three days to understand how rough the Earth is. What happened in Japan, with the Great East Japan Earthquake, tells us how strong a tsunami can actually be. It's not only about the tsunami; that tsunami is connected to countless other occurrences. In Japan they say things such as: 'We built this wall 1 km from the coast. So, nothing will ever happen to it.' But something will happen. Danger is fantastic. And I believe we live in an incredibly interesting time. Words such as danger and risk are as much a part of architecture as anything else.

PROMPTER

Danger and risk can exert a fascination because they often leave the outgoing open, and they concentrate on the process itself. To which extent do you include danger and risk in your understanding of creating?

THE ARCHITECT

We have to talk about our discipline in a relative way. When I described the 'body hotel' in the book *Stills*, I began by explaining

that the hospital has become a completely different environment from what we once knew. We now have to take illness and disease as part of life. We must not exclude death. We should not purely rationalize it. But from our society. Within the last thirty years, everyone has been so interested in the body, and the fact that we can, more than ever before, control it. Previously only a minority were interested in disease, illness, or death. But these acts are all simply part of life. Like in Mexico, where the skull is part of life, living with death, is something we seem to be traumatized by. We will continue to discover new knowledge about the world, but soon we will also live and experience life on Mars and travel into orbit and look back at our great Mother Earth, and potentially see it as only a neighborhood in the universe. My father died in the first decade of the 2000s, and afterward I realized how such an experience could have such a severe effects for those left behind. Only then did I understand, for the first time, why the people in Mexico 500 or 600 years ago, celebrated death the way they did. They played games, where one challenged another, and where the winner would have his heart taken out. Where you are challenged to win, you are challenged to die. That's something I like very much. I've been to Mexico many times, and have always wondered how their culture could be so positive toward the subject of death. When we speak about Unconscious City, death is an extremely important issue to ponder. We must be aware of its coming. When we speak about the Unconscious City, we can only be serious about it, when we are aware of death. I enjoy thinking about the city, a new city that accepts disease and fear, as well as risk and death. I call this city, the Unconscious City.

08:19:30

08:24:00

足立480
さ 73-03
8

6
ENEOS
5
コーティング技術認定店
KeePer
PRO SHOP
キーパープロショップ

VISA
もんじゃ
Mighty Vision
F21
FOREVER 2
GALAXY Tab
大盛堂書店

Author
Wiel Arets, Amsterdam

Editor
John Bezold, Amsterdam

Graphic Design
Mainstudio, Edwin van Gelder, Amsterdam

Printing
Lenoirschuring, Amsterdam

Binding
Patist, Den Dolder

Publisher
Actar Publishers
355 Lexington Ave, 8th Floor
New York, NY 10017, USA
Phone +1 212 966 2207
salesnewyork@actar-d.com
eurosales@actar-d.com

Paper
IBO One and Neobond

Typefaces
Stanley and Monospace 821

A CIP catalogue record for this book is available from the Library of Congress, Washington D.C., USA.

ISBN: 9781945150654

Library of Congress
Control Number: 2017952483

Cover: Wiel Arets, Gion, Kyoto, 1993
Portrait: Wiel Arets by Nobuyoshi Araki, Tokyo, 2006
All other photographs in this book were taken by Wiel Arets during numerous trips to Japan, during the period of 2010-2018, in Tokyo, in Nishi-Azabu, Minato-ku, Tsukiji, Chūō-ku, Roppongi, Shinjuku-ku, Ginza, Shibuya-ku, Chiyoda-ku, and Kita-Aoyama.

This book originated from a series of lectures and interviews with Wiel Arets at the Berlin University of the Arts, Germany–conducted by Julian Schubert, Leonard Streich, and Elena Schütz, with the assistance of Elsa Katharina Jacobi–during his time as Professor of Building Planning and Design, from 2004-2012. Further conversations took place between others and Arets in the period 2013-2018, in Amsterdam, Chicago, New York City, Montreal, and Tokyo, which were then condensed, edited, and combined with the prior interviews from Berlin–creating a truly global conversation.

This publication has been made possible with the support of the Berlin University of the Arts.

Printed and bound in the Netherlands.

wielaretsarchitects.com

The following script of thoughts was used to organize this publication's chapters. It is included here in order to relay the original thoughts that eventually led to this final publication. Similar to the first sketch of a building, which is always different than its completed state; this script serves as the first sketch of this publication, thus documenting the making of this book, during its eight years of development.

PREFACE

Why are so many books made, even more, than before the idea of a paperless society?

A. Why is this book of any relevance, and for whom it is written?

B. *Vers une Architecture* (machine), *L'Architettura della Citta* (monument), *Delirious New York* (phenomena).

C. Research, Intuition, Zeitgeist.

D. The dialogue... Plato, Valéry, Cattaneo...

E. History... Generations... Role of the professors and their students...

F. AA, Columbia, Berlage Institute, UdK, Princeton, Cooper Union...

G. Speculation, no utopias.

H. Songlines, as a strategy.

UNCONSCIOUS

Processing perception, memory, learning, thought, and language without awareness.

A. What is the Unconscious City? Urban plan of Barcelona, versus the chaos of Tokyo; physical, versus immaterial; realism, versus surrealism.

B. What is the position of the city, the metropolis, and the megacity, within the next seventy-five years?

C. Borders, within the city, but also at its edge.

D. Hierarchy, Diversity, Multi-center, Living-Working through the pattern of...

E. What... will it look... like? 3-D...

F. Un-control... un-like... un-un-un-un...

G. Who is in charge... mayor/politics... media... financial system...?

H. Megapolis... the rest of the mainland, including the jungle, and the...

I. BeSeTo and other... Strong-lines... Networks...

J. What will be, the position of the village?

K. Formal, versus informal...

L. Economic values, versus other values... Property-value... How to bring production back into the city... Venice, Brooklyn, Monjuïc, and Montparnasse...

The following script of thoughts was used to organize this publication's chapters. It is included here in order to relay the original thoughts that eventually led to this final publication. Similar to the first sketch of a building, which is always different than its completed state; this script serves as the first sketch of this publication, thus documenting the making of this book, during its eight years of development.

PREFACE

Why are so many books made, even more, than before the idea of a paperless society?

A. Why is this book of any relevance, and for whom it is written?
B. Vers une Architecture (machine), L'Architettura della Citta (monument), Delirious New York (phenomena).
C. Research, Intuition, Zeitgeist.
D. The dialogue... Plato, Valéry, Cattaneo...
E. History... Generations... Role of the professors and their students...
F. AA, Columbia, Berlage Institute, UdK, Princeton, Cooper Union...
G. Speculation, no utopias.
H. Songlines, as a strategy.

UNCONSCIOUS

Processing perception, memory, learning, thought, and language without awareness.

A. What is the Unconscious City? Urban plan of Barcelona, versus the chaos of Tokyo; physical, versus immaterial; realism, versus surrealism.
B. What is the position of the city, the metropolis, and the megacity, within the next seventy-five years?
C. Borders, within the city, but also at its edge.
D. Hierarchy, Diversity, Multi-center, Living-Working through the pattern of...
E. What... will it look... like? 3-D...
F. Un-control... un-like... un-un-un-un...
G. Who is in charge... mayor/politics... media... financial system...?
H. Megapolis... the rest of the mainland, including the jungle, and the...
I. BeSeTo and other... Strong-lines... Networks...
J. What will be, the position of the village?
K. Formal, versus informal...
L. Economic values, versus other values... Property-value... How to bring production back into the city... Venice, Brooklyn, Montjuïc, and Montparnasse...

COUNTRYSIDE

When the city stops, the countryside begins.

A. Nature, jungle...
B. Humans, versus animals and plants.
C. Tourism...
D. Oil, wood, gold...
E. Fishing, and hunting.
F. Who, exactly, owns what...
G. Orbit, Moon, Mars, Venus.

ARBEITER

Individuals are responsible for their own actions and governments cannot be blamed.

A. Ernst Jünger...
B. Moon... Computer... Robot... Creative... Multiply...
C. Free... and... Independent...
D. ...the collective...
E. Religion, versus sports...
F. Media-dominance.
G. Child-Student-Worker-Pension?
H. Still heroes?... Bill Gates, Madonna, Steve Jobs? ...Are there more; why?...

INFRA

How do humans physically and mentally move?

A. Paul Virilio... Mother and child, versus... Magnitude 4.5...
B. Physical distance... versus, digital distance...
C. Plane-Train-Car-Bike-Foot. Or...?
D. Seventy-two minutes...
E. Traffic-knots... versus, other programs...
F. Comfort... Megapolis... Cemetery... Style? World? Ocean?
G. How do we communicate...
H. Do we lose time, while traveling?
I. Why do we not communicate with other passengers, when riding the subway?

PROGRAM

A sequence of instructions.

A. The city as a cross-section, of roads and rivers, trading point, gathering exchange...
B. The city, was the collective memory.

C. The city, for death. Egypt... Mexico...
D. Egypt... Greece... Rome... Middle Ages... Defense... Renaissance... Industrial Revolution... Nineteenth-century... The Modern Movement... Tokyo... Megapolis.
E. Life, versus living, housing, versus working.
F. Production, in the city.
G. Shopping... Department store, versus boutique... Fast, versus chef...
H. Culture?
I. Music and film...
J. House, shop, library, factory, museum, church...
K. The book, the magazine... versus... digital media...

UN-C-C

Cities must prepare for the radical changes to come.

A. The street, and the public realm.
B. What will differentiate cities on each continent?
C. Is 'our/the neighbor', still an issue?
D. The impact of the iPhone, it is as big a paradigm shift, as the Industrial Revolution.
E. What is the position of death, within our society?
F. The human body, versus the human intellect.
G. Cultural differences... multi-what... but, as a quality...
H. War... Anonymous... Outlaws... Gangs... The Mafia...
I. Fashion... Writing... Thomas Mann...
J. Events... Olympic Games... City, as a brand...
K. To be organized... to survive...
L. Restaurants and bars... food and drink... transforming moments...
M. Do we still want to marry...? Do we still want children...? How do we organize our family...? How to organize sex, and excitement...? Kabukichō.
N. How will we perceive the megapolis, and how can the city, prepare for its future?

URBANIZATION

The process by which people resettle to live in urban areas.

A. What will be the position of urban disciplines?
B. Will 'the appearance', still be of any relevance?
C. Do we still consider the icon to be relevant?
D. Materials to build with... Glass... Steel... Artificial components...?
E. Technology.
F. Durability.

G. Multiple addresses. We no longer live in one place: Street address-Internet address.
H. Public and private... in our homes we are different people, than online. New naked.
I. Why are Malaparte, and Luis Barragán, interesting architects...?

POSTSCRIPT/CV

Why is Wiel Arets, since his youth, interested in the Moon?
A. Who, exactly, is Wiel Arets?
B. What, exactly, did and does, he do?
C. Who are his companions... Mies, Valéry, Mapplethorpe, Godard...
D. Why does he tend to wear Comme des Garçons?
E. Why has he chosen, to live in multiple cities?
F. Why does he prefer, to drive a Porsche 911?
G. Why is involvement in academia, next to his studio practice, important for him?
H. Why he is successful, and what, exactly, are his own unconscious dilemmas?
I. Why did he ask Julian Schubert, Elena Schütz, and Leonard Streich to have this dialogue?

Wiel Arets (1955) is a Dutch architect whose critical thinking and intense interest in physics, philosophy, cinema, literature, and the human condition informs every level of his life and work. He established Wiel Arets Architects (WAA) in 1983, the same year he first visited Japan–the topic around which this book is organized. During his studies at the Technical University of Eindhoven, his MSc thesis explored the idea of 'The Architecture of Freedom'; while teaching as the Diplom Unit One Master at the AA London, 'Void' was the focus of the research; thereafter, at Columbia University and the Cooper Union New York, his research centered on the theme 'Virological Architecture'. During 2004-2012, as Professor of Building Planning and Design at the Berlin University of the Arts, he focused 'Studio Arets' on 'A Wonderful World: A New Map of the World'. From 2012-2017, he was Dean of the College of Architecture at the Illinois Institute of Technology in Chicago–where his approach was 'Nowness'; the school was structured around the idea of 'Rethinking Metropolis'–where he remains a tenured architecture professor. Wiel Arets Architects is organized around the core principle of making; with its globally renowned built oeuvre, which is widely published, it has, from its onset, concentrated on the making of architecture, urbanism, research, books, and industrial design.